About the Author

David Webb holds a first-class honors degree in psychology and a Master's degree in Occupational Psychology. For several years, David was a lecturer in psychology at the University of Huddersfield in the United Kingdom.

As the owner, writer, and host of three influential websites, David has harnessed his teaching and research expertise to reach a global audience. Among his online ventures, All-About-Psychology.Com stands out as a premier resource, attracting over two million visitors annually.

David Webb is also a bestselling author, with a portfolio that includes notable works such as 'The Psychology Student Guide,' 'The Incredibly Interesting Psychology Book,' and 'On This Day in Psychology.' His written contributions have not only enriched the understanding of psychology but have also made the subject more accessible to a wide readership.

David's passionate promotion of psychology online is underscored by his social media presence. With over one million followers across various platforms, he continues to inspire and engage fellow psychology enthusiasts worldwide. In his role as an educator, author, and online advocate for psychology, David Webb remains committed to fostering curiosity, knowledge, and passion for this captivating field.

For my amazing sons, Luca and Paolo.

I think psychology is the most interesting of all fields. It's the most interesting because it's about us. It's about the most important and intimate aspects of our lives. It's about language and perception, it's about our memory of things. It's about our dreams, love and hate. It's about morality, our sense of right and wrong. It's about when things go wrong as in depression, our anxiety. It's about happiness. It's about everything that matters to us.

Professor Paul Bloom

Contents

Introduction

Hello, I'm David Webb, a former university lecturer in psychology, and I'm delighted to welcome you to *"Psychology Q & A: Great Answers to Fascinating Questions."*

In March 2008, I launched All-About-Psychology.Com with the aim of providing comprehensive psychology information and resources to anyone, regardless of their connection to the subject – whether they are a student, educator, professional or simply have a general interest in psychology. As part of this mission, I introduced a knowledge-sharing initiative, allowing visitors to ask or answer psychology questions. Since its inception, this section of the website has received over 2000 submissions, and the content of the book is drawn directly from these submissions.

As you navigate through the book, each question is presented in italics, accompanied by a clear and concise answer. There is no order to the questions, so feel free to jump to any of them that capture your attention. It is my sincere hope that each question posed and its corresponding answer will not only satisfy your curiosity but also ignite your passion for further learning. To facilitate this, some entries include links to additional information on the All About Psychology website, allowing you to delve deeper and expand your knowledge. For psychology students in search of research project or final year dissertation ideas, reading this book will provide you with a wealth of inspiration.

Before you dive into your first psychology Q & A, please take a moment to connect with me and join over a million fellow psychology enthusiasts through my social media channels.

facebook.com/psychologyonline

twitter.com/psych101

pinterest.com/psychology

linkedin.com/groups/4016322 (Psychology Students Network)

youtube.com/@LearnAboutPsychology

tumblr.com/all-about-psychology

instagram.com/allaboutpsychology

You can stay up-to-date with all the latest information and resources on the All About Psychology website by subscribing to the All About Psychology newsletter. Here's the link:

bit.ly/AllAboutPsychNews

If you find value in this book and enjoy the journey it takes you on, I would be very grateful if you would consider leaving a review on Amazon. You can help support the All About Psychology website by visiting the All About Psychology Amazon Store.

amazon.com/shop/psychologyonline

Thank you so much, your support means the world to me.

Finally, please bear in mind that none of the content in this book should be considered a substitute for professional psychological, psychiatric or medial advice, diagnosis or treatment.

Fake News

Why do people believe fake news?

Here are some of the most compelling reasons why people might believe fake news:

Cognitive Biases: Human brains are subject to various cognitive biases that can make us more susceptible to fake news. Confirmation bias, for example, leads us to seek information that confirms our existing beliefs, making us more likely to accept information that aligns with our preconceived notions.

Emotional Appeal: Fake news often relies on emotional triggers. Stories that evoke strong emotions, such as fear, anger, or excitement, tend to be more memorable and persuasive. People may be more likely to believe information that resonates with their emotions.

Social Confirmation: People tend to trust information that comes from their social networks. If a piece of news is shared by friends or family, it may be perceived as more credible, even if it is false. Social media platforms amplify this effect.

Limited Media Literacy: Not everyone possesses strong media literacy skills. Some individuals may have difficulty distinguishing between credible and non-credible sources. They may lack the critical thinking skills needed to evaluate the reliability of information.

Information Overload: In the digital age, people are inundated with information from various sources. This can lead to information overload and a decreased ability to discern between trustworthy and untrustworthy sources. People may rely on heuristics (mental shortcuts), such as the reputation of the source, to make quick judgments.

Echo Chambers: Online communities and social media can create echo chambers where people are exposed only to information that reinforces their existing beliefs. This can lead to the reinforcement of false or misleading information within these closed networks.

Misperception of Trustworthiness: Fake news can be designed to mimic the appearance of legitimate news sources, making it difficult to distinguish from credible information. People may inadvertently trust misleading content because it looks professional.

Desire for Sensationalism: Sensational or sensationalized news stories are often more attention-grabbing. People may be drawn to stories that are shocking, unusual, or provocative, making them more susceptible to believing false information.

Political and Ideological Motivations: Fake news is sometimes disseminated to advance a political agenda or ideology. Individuals who strongly identify with a particular group or ideology may be more inclined to accept information that supports their worldview.

Lack of Time: People are busy, and they may not have the time to fact-check every piece of information they encounter. This can lead to a reliance on shortcuts, such as accepting information at face value.

Overconfidence: Some individuals may overestimate their ability to detect fake news. This overconfidence can make them more susceptible to misinformation because they believe they are immune to its effects.

In an era of information overload and the rapid spread of information through various media channels, it is essential for individuals to be aware of the cognitive and social factors that can influence their beliefs and decisions. Encouraging people to be vigilant in evaluating the information they encounter requires a varied approach that includes media literacy education, critical thinking skills development, and efforts to promote trustworthy journalism.

Freudian Defense Mechanism

Could someone please explain in simple terms what a Freudian defense mechanism is and provide a good example.

In psychology, defense mechanisms are ways that our mind uses to protect itself from uncomfortable or distressing thoughts, feelings, or memories. Sigmund Freud, the famous psychoanalyst, proposed several defense mechanisms as a part of his theory of the mind.

These mechanisms work at an unconscious level, meaning we are not usually aware that we're using them. They help us cope with anxiety and protect our self-esteem, but they can also distort reality to some extent.

Denial

One of the most straightforward defense mechanisms is denial. When someone is in denial, they refuse to accept the reality of a situation because facing it would be too uncomfortable. They may ignore or reject evidence that contradicts their belief.

Example: Imagine someone who smokes heavily and knows that it's harmful to their health. They may constantly tell themselves and others that smoking doesn't really cause any health problems, despite overwhelming evidence to the contrary. They might avoid going to the doctor for check-ups to prevent hearing bad news about their health.

In this case, the person is using denial as a defense mechanism to protect themselves from the anxiety and guilt associated with the knowledge that their behavior is harmful. It allows them to maintain a sense of comfort and avoid the distressing reality that they should quit smoking for their well-being.

It's important to note that while defense mechanisms can be adaptive in certain situations, they can also be maladaptive if overused. They can prevent individuals from dealing with problems effectively and may lead to psychological distress. In psychoanalysis, part of the therapeutic process involves helping individuals become more aware of and manage these defense mechanisms to promote healthier psychological functioning.

Related Information on The All About Psychology Website

Learn all about the profoundly influential life, work and legacy of Sigmund Freud.

www.all-about-psychology.com/sigmund-freud.html

Learn all about psychoanalysis.

www.all-about-psychology.com/psychoanalysis.html

What Does Sensory Deprivation Do to a Person

What are the psychological after effects of 96 hours light, sound, and human contact deprivation?

Sensory deprivation, particularly when it involves the absence of light, sound, and human contact for an extended period like 96 hours, can have profound psychological effects on individuals. These effects can vary depending on factors such as individual susceptibility, pre-existing psychological conditions, and personal coping mechanisms. Here are 10 potential psychological after effects of such deprivation:

1. Hallucinations and Distorted Perceptions: Prolonged sensory deprivation can lead to sensory distortions and hallucinations. The absence of external stimuli can cause the brain to generate its own sensory experiences, leading to visual, auditory, or even tactile hallucinations. These experiences can be vivid and unsettling.

2. Cognitive Disturbances: Individuals subjected to sensory deprivation may experience cognitive disturbances such as difficulties in concentration, memory lapses, and impaired problem-solving abilities. The lack of sensory input that the brain relies on for cognitive processing can disrupt normal cognitive functioning.

3. Emotional Instability: Isolation from external sensory experiences and human interaction can contribute to emotional instability. Feelings of anxiety, depression, irritability, and even emotional numbness can emerge as a result of the prolonged sensory deprivation.

4. Anxiety and Panic: The absence of external stimuli can lead to heightened awareness of internal bodily sensations, potentially inducing anxiety or even panic attacks. Individuals might become hyper-focused on their physiological processes, leading to increased heart rate, rapid breathing, and other anxiety-related symptoms.

5. Altered Time Perception: Sensory deprivation can distort individuals' perception of time. Without external cues like daylight or auditory cues, individuals might struggle to accurately track time, leading to feelings of timelessness or disorientation.

6. Changes in Sleep Patterns: Deprivation of natural light and sound cues can disrupt circadian rhythms and sleep patterns. Individuals might experience difficulties falling asleep, staying asleep, or experiencing restorative sleep.

7. Self-Reflection and Introspection: In the absence of external distractions, some individuals might engage in deep self-reflection and introspection. This can lead to profound insights but might also exacerbate feelings of loneliness or existential distress.

8. Decreased Social Skills: Extended isolation from human contact can lead to a decline in social skills and an increased sense of social awkwardness. Interpersonal interactions might become challenging after such deprivation.

9. Sensory Overload After Release: When individuals are reintroduced to sensory stimuli after prolonged deprivation, they might experience sensory overload. Ordinary sensations might feel overwhelming, leading to anxiety or discomfort.

10. Coping Mechanisms: Different individuals respond differently to sensory deprivation. Some might develop coping mechanisms such as daydreaming, fantasy, or creating imaginary scenarios to counteract the lack of external stimuli.

It's important to note that while sensory deprivation research has provided valuable insights into the potential effects of extreme isolation, conducting such experiments raises ethical concerns due to the potential harm it can cause. Researchers must prioritize the well-being and mental health of participants and adhere to ethical guidelines when studying sensory deprivation.

Ultimately, the psychological after effects of 96 hours of light, sound, and human contact deprivation can range from sensory distortions and emotional instability to altered cognitive functioning and disrupted sleep patterns. These effects underscore the profound impact that sensory input and social interaction have on human psychological well-being.

Narcissistic Personality

I think one of my friends has a narcissistic personality. I have known him for over a year and he has often struck me with his "peculiar" reactions to events and to my own behavior, to the point that I began wondering if I was normal. Fortunately, my other friends confirmed that they would feel the same as me, if they were in my shoes. I tried telling him how much I was feeling let down by him but all I got was "calm down for your own sake". So I decided to end our friendship.

I then came across an article on narcissistic personality disorder and now most of his reactions make sense. He was hypersensitive to criticism, a perfectionist (which he showed with unconcealed pride) and always constantly telling me about his achievements. The thing is, I now feel a bit sorry for him and wonder whether I should try helping him. I am aware I will get nothing out of it (my other friends say I am playing the good nun!); but no longer being his friend will teach him nothing and only add to his problems. What I would like to know is, how can I best help and support him.

I appreciate your concern for your friend and your willingness to understand and support them. However, assuming your friend does have narcissistic personality disorder (having narcissistic traits doesn't automatically mean a person has narcissistic personality disorder), it's important to approach this situation with caution, as dealing with individuals with narcissistic traits or narcissistic personality disorder can be complex. Here are some considerations to keep in mind:

Self-Care First: While your intention to help is admirable, it's crucial to prioritize your own well-being. Narcissistic individuals can have a significant impact on the emotional well-being of those around them. Make sure you establish healthy boundaries and ensure your own emotional health is not compromised.

Seek Professional Guidance: Narcissistic personality traits can be deeply ingrained and challenging to address without professional help. Encourage your friend to seek therapy from a mental health professional who specializes in personality disorders. However, remember that individuals with narcissistic traits often have difficulty recognizing their own issues and seeking help.

Empathetic Communication: If you choose to engage with your friend, approach them with empathy and compassion. Use "I" statements to express your concerns and feelings. For example, say, "I've noticed that our interactions have sometimes felt challenging for me, and I wanted to talk about it."

Avoid Blame or Criticism: Narcissistic individuals can be highly sensitive to criticism. Focus on sharing your observations rather than blaming or accusing. Keep in mind that they may not respond well initially.

Set Realistic Expectations: Changing narcissistic behavior is a long and complex process. Be prepared for resistance or denial. Your friend may not be ready to acknowledge their behavior or seek help.

Educate Yourself Further: Understanding narcissistic traits and behaviors can help you approach the situation with greater understanding and patience. It can also help you manage your own expectations and emotions.

Focus on Positive Qualities: While narcissistic individuals may display challenging behaviors, they often have positive qualities as well. Acknowledge and appreciate their strengths when you can.

Encourage Self-Reflection: If your friend is open to it, encourage self-reflection. Ask open-ended questions that might lead them to consider their behavior and its impact on others.

Support from Afar: You mentioned that you've ended your friendship with this person. If you decide not to re-establish the friendship, you can still provide support from a distance. Send well wishes, share resources, and let them know you care about their well-being.

Understand Your Limits: It's important to recognize that you may not be able to change your friend's behavior. People can only change if they themselves recognize the need for change and are motivated to do so.

Remember that your primary responsibility is to yourself and your well-being. Offering support is admirable, but it's also important to recognize when your efforts are not having a positive impact. It's ultimately up to your friend to take the initiative to address their own behaviors and seek help if needed.

Related Information on The All About Psychology Website

www.all-about-psychology.com/narcissists.html

Narcissists: There's More Than One Type – And Our Research Reveals What Makes Each Tick. Insightful article by Nikhila Mahadevan, Lecturer in Psychology at the University of Essex.

www.all-about-psychology.com/types-of-narcissist.html

How Many Types of Narcissist Are There? A Psychology Expert Sets the

Record Straight. Excellent article by Dr. Megan Willis.

Psychology of Escapism

Psychologically speaking, what is escapist behavior?

Escapist behavior refers to actions or strategies that individuals employ to avoid facing or dealing with reality, particularly when they are confronted with stress, discomfort, emotional challenges, or responsibilities. This behavior often involves seeking distraction, disengagement, or detachment from the demands of everyday life. Psychologically, it can be understood through several perspectives:

Coping Mechanism: Escapist behavior can serve as a coping mechanism in response to stress or overwhelming emotions. It provides individuals with a temporary escape from their problems or emotional distress, offering relief or distraction.

Avoidance Behavior: From a psychological standpoint, escapism can be seen as a form of avoidance behavior. It involves evading or postponing dealing with uncomfortable or anxiety-provoking situations, which can lead to short-term relief but may exacerbate long-term problems.

Fantasy and Imagination: Escapism often involves engaging in fantasies, daydreams, or immersive activities like reading, gaming, or watching movies or TV shows. This engagement allows individuals to temporarily detach from their immediate reality and immerse themselves in alternate worlds or scenarios.

Mood Regulation: Escapist behaviors may also serve to regulate mood. For instance, consuming substances like alcohol or drugs or engaging in excessive entertainment can alter one's emotional state temporarily, providing a sense of relief or pleasure.

Social Isolation: Escapism can manifest as social withdrawal or isolation. Some individuals may avoid social interactions and responsibilities by retreating into solitude, which can have both positive and negative psychological consequences.

Maladaptive vs. Adaptive Escapism: Escapist behaviors can be categorized as either maladaptive or adaptive. Maladaptive escapism involves behaviors that harm one's well-being or hinder personal growth. Adaptive escapism, on the other hand, includes activities that provide a healthy break from stress or emotional challenges, such as exercising, practicing mindfulness, or engaging in creative hobbies.

Impact on Mental Health: Escapism can impact mental health positively or negatively. In the short term, it may alleviate stress, but if relied upon excessively, it can lead to avoidance of problems, emotional repression, and the neglect of important responsibilities, which may contribute to mental health issues.

Individual Differences: The nature and impact of escapism can vary significantly among individuals. What one person considers a healthy form of escape, another may view as problematic or detrimental to their well-being.

It's important to recognize that some degree of escapism is a normal and healthy part of life. Everyone needs breaks from stressors and challenges. However, when escapism becomes the primary way of coping with life's demands, it can lead to negative consequences. Balancing healthy forms of escapism with facing life's challenges directly and seeking support when needed is crucial for psychological well-being. If escapism is causing significant disruption or distress in one's life, consulting with a mental health professional can be beneficial in exploring healthier coping strategies and addressing underlying issues.

Negativity Bias

Why do people tend to dwell on negative things rather than positive things.

People tend to dwell on negative things more than positive ones due to several cognitive biases and psychological mechanisms. Here are some of the main reasons:

Negativity Bias: The negativity bias is a well-documented cognitive bias that suggests people give more weight to negative information and experiences than positive ones. This bias likely has evolutionary roots; our ancestors who paid more attention to potential threats and dangers were more likely to survive. Consequently, our brains are wired to be more sensitive to negative stimuli.

Emotional Intensity: Negative emotions tend to be more intense and attention-grabbing than positive emotions. For example, fear, anger, and sadness often feel stronger and demand more cognitive processing than happiness or contentment. This heightened emotional intensity can lead people to dwell on negative experiences.

Adaptive Function: Dwellings on negative experiences can serve an adaptive function. It helps us learn from our mistakes and avoid potentially harmful situations in the future. This learning process has been crucial for human survival and development.

Memory Formation: Negative events are often remembered more vividly and for longer periods than positive events. This phenomenon is known as memory bias. For example, people are more likely to remember a traumatic event or a personal failure in great detail compared to a joyful celebration.

Self-Protection: Reflecting on negative experiences can be a form of self-protection. By focusing on potential threats or mistakes, individuals may attempt to avoid repeating them, which can lead to better decision-making and risk management.

Cultural and Social Influence: Cultural and societal factors can also play a role. Some cultures and societies place a greater emphasis on negative feedback and criticism, reinforcing the tendency to dwell on negative aspects.

Rumination: Rumination is the act of repeatedly thinking about the same thoughts or problems, often with a negative or distressing focus. This cognitive habit can lead individuals to dwell on negative experiences, exacerbating their impact on mental well-being.

Selective Attention: People may unconsciously pay more attention to negative information in their environment. For instance, in a sea of compliments and positive feedback, one piece of criticism can dominate a person's thoughts.

While the inclination to dwell on negative things is a natural aspect of human psychology, it's essential to strike a balance. Excessive rumination on negative thoughts can contribute to stress, anxiety, and even depression. To mitigate this bias, individuals can practice mindfulness, gratitude, and positive psychology techniques to foster a more balanced perspective and improve mental well-being.

Left Brain Vs. Right Brain

Is it true that the left side of the brain is especially adapted for the production and understanding of speech, while the right side of the brain is especially adapted for handling perceptual skills, such as drawing a picture or recognizing melodies?

The concept of hemispheric specialization, often referred to as "lateralization of brain function," suggests that certain cognitive functions are predominantly localized in one hemisphere of the brain. While it is true that the brain's left and right hemispheres are not identical in their functions, the popular notion of a clear-cut division between "logical left" and "creative right" is somewhat oversimplified.

Here are some general tendencies of hemispheric specialization:

Language Processing: In most right-handed individuals and many left-handed individuals, language processing is largely localized in the left hemisphere, particularly in areas like Broca's area and Wernicke's area. These regions play crucial roles in speech production and language comprehension, respectively. However, it's essential to note that language processing is a complex function involving networks across both hemispheres, and some aspects of language processing can involve the right hemisphere.

Perceptual and Spatial Skills: The right hemisphere is generally associated with perceptual and spatial skills, such as recognizing faces, interpreting emotions, and understanding spatial relationships. It is also involved in processing nonverbal cues and visual imagery.

Motor Skills: While not directly related to the question, it's worth mentioning that the left hemisphere is responsible for controlling the right side of the body, and the right hemisphere controls the left side of the body. This crossed control is due to the way nerves in the brainstem connect to the opposite side of the body.

Individual Differences: It's important to emphasize that hemispheric specialization can vary among individuals. Some people may exhibit greater lateralization of specific functions, while others may show more bilateral distribution of those functions.

Plasticity and Complexity: The brain is incredibly adaptive and plastic, meaning that functions can be redistributed to different brain areas to some extent, especially after injury or during developmental processes.

It's essential to avoid overly rigid assumptions about the functions of each hemisphere, as the brain operates through interconnected networks, and most cognitive processes involve the collaboration of both hemispheres.

Additionally, handedness can also influence hemispheric specialization. For example, left-handed individuals may show different patterns of lateralization compared to right-handed individuals.

In summary, while certain cognitive functions tend to be associated with specific brain hemispheres, the brain's actual organization is much more complex, and numerous factors influence how various functions are distributed and interact within the brain. The field of neuropsychology continues to investigate these complexities to gain a more comprehensive understanding of brain function and lateralization.

Related Information on The All About Psychology Website

www.all-about-psychology.com/left-brain-right-brain-myth.html

Why The Left-Brain Right-Brain Myth Will Probably Never Die Excellent article by psychologist, award-winning writer and best selling author Dr Christian Jarrett.

Dealing With Critical People

My Mom is one of the critical people in my life. She and others have only negative concerns to express about my goals and plans. When I plan a trip out of state, she and others say, "What if so and so..." or "How are you going to do that?" They don't even realize the negativity they exude when they come back at me with these critiques of what I have in mind. How do I keep them from discouraging me and thus holding me back?

It can be incredibly challenging and disheartening when the people closest to us, such as your Mom and others, consistently express negative concerns and critiques about our goals and plans. Dealing with unsupportive or critical individuals can indeed feel discouraging and may impact your motivation and confidence in pursuing your dreams. Here are some strategies you can consider to handle this situation:

Open Communication: Have a candid and honest conversation with your Mom and others about how their negative remarks affect you. Express your feelings and let them know that you value their input, but you also need their support and encouragement in pursuing your goals.

Set Boundaries: Politely let them know that while you appreciate their concern, you would prefer to discuss your plans with them after you have thought things through and made your decisions. Set boundaries to protect yourself from constant negativity.

Find Supportive Individuals: Seek out other people who are more supportive and encouraging of your goals and aspirations. Surrounding yourself with positive influences can uplift and motivate you, making it easier to pursue your dreams despite the discouragement from others.

Believe in Yourself: Remember that your goals and plans are important to you, and it's essential to have faith in yourself and your abilities. Don't let the negativity of others undermine your self-confidence.

Address Their Concerns: If your Mom and others have genuine concerns about your plans, take the time to listen and understand their perspective. You can address their worries by providing well-thought-out solutions or contingency plans.

Focus on Positive Reinforcement: Surround yourself with positive affirmations and reminders of your strengths and capabilities. Visualize yourself achieving your goals and draw inspiration from your vision of success.

Seek Professional Guidance: If the criticism and negativity from your Mom and others are significantly affecting your well-being and confidence, consider seeking support from a therapist or counselor. A mental health professional can help you navigate these challenges and build resilience.

Prove Yourself through Actions: As you move forward with your plans, let your actions and accomplishments speak for themselves. Showing progress and success can sometimes change the perspectives of others, including those who were initially critical.

Practice Self-Care: Taking care of your mental and emotional well-being is crucial. Engage in activities that bring you joy, manage stress, and prioritize self-care. When you feel emotionally resilient, it becomes easier to handle criticism and negativity.

Remember that it's essential to stay true to yourself and pursue what brings you fulfillment and happiness. You have the right to follow your dreams, and although the negative opinions of others can be hurtful, they don't define your worth or potential. Stay focused on your goals, seek support from those who uplift you, and don't be afraid to set healthy boundaries with unsupportive individuals. Your determination and resilience can lead you to success despite the challenges you encounter along the way.

Psychology of the Criminally Insane

I'm very interested in the psychology of the Criminally Insane, as it intrigues me how the human mind works, and why certain people behave the way they do. I would love to learn know more about the subject, so if anybody has any information on this topic, I would be grateful if they could share it, along with any online resources.

The study of the psychology of the criminally insane is a captivating and controversial field that delves into the intersection of mental illness and criminal behavior. It involves understanding the minds of individuals who commit crimes while also displaying significant signs of mental disorder. Over the years, this field has evolved, influenced by advancements in psychology, sociology, criminology, law, psychiatry, and societal attitudes toward mental health.

Historical Context:

Early Notions: The concept of criminal insanity dates back to ancient times, where individuals were often considered possessed by evil spirits or punished by the divine for their actions.

Emergence of Psychiatry: In the 19th century, with the rise of modern psychiatry, there was a shift toward understanding criminal behavior from a medical perspective. The work of figures like Philippe Pinel and Dorothea Dix laid the foundation for recognizing mental illness as a factor in criminal conduct.

Development of Key Concepts:

M'Naghten Rule (1843): The trial of Daniel M'Naghten in England led to the establishment of the M'Naghten Rule, which focused on whether a defendant could distinguish right from wrong due to mental illness. This became a landmark in the insanity defense.

The Durkheim Era: Emile Durkheim's sociological theories contributed to a broader understanding of the social factors influencing criminal behavior. This era emphasized societal elements that could contribute to mental illness and crime.

Modern Forensic Psychology: In the 20th century, forensic psychology emerged as a distinct field, focusing on the interface between psychology and the legal system. Professionals began to assess the mental state of individuals involved in criminal cases, including those deemed criminally insane.

Contemporary Approaches:

Diagnostic and Statistical Manual (DSM): The DSM, published by the American Psychiatric Association, provides standardized criteria for diagnosing mental disorders. This has been crucial in evaluating the mental health of individuals involved in criminal cases.

Insanity Defense Reforms: Many legal systems have reformed their insanity defense criteria over time. These reforms aim to strike a balance between recognizing mental illness as a factor while ensuring that individuals who are truly criminally responsible are held accountable.

Advances in Neuroscience: Modern neuroscience has provided insights into the neurological basis of certain behaviors and mental disorders. Brain imaging techniques have contributed to understanding the brain mechanisms associated with criminal behavior and mental illness.

Treatment and Rehabilitation: Contemporary approaches also emphasize the importance of mental health treatment and rehabilitation for individuals with mental disorders who have committed crimes. These approaches aim to address the underlying causes of criminal behavior and reduce recidivism.

The history and development of the psychology of the criminally insane have evolved from ancient notions of possession to a multidisciplinary approach that combines psychology, law, psychiatry, and societal considerations. Understanding the minds of those who commit crimes while grappling with mental illness is a dynamic and evolving field that continues to shape legal and mental health practices worldwide.

Useful Links

www.all-about-forensic-psychology.com

www.all-about-forensic-psychology.com/insanity-defense.html

Asking for a Friend

Is there a term for when people pretend to get advice for a "friend" when the advice is really for them? And what are the psychological issues at play when someone is reluctant to admit that they need help with a problem?

The behavior of seeking advice for oneself but disguising it as seeking advice for a "friend" is commonly referred to as "proxy seeking" or "proxy question asking." This term describes the act of presenting a personal issue or concern as if it pertains to someone else to maintain a sense of anonymity or to avoid vulnerability. Proxy seeking is not uncommon, and it can be an indication of certain psychological issues at play:

Fear of Judgment or Stigma: Some individuals may be reluctant to admit they need help due to a fear of being judged, criticized, or stigmatized for their problems. By posing the question as if it's for a friend, they can gauge reactions without revealing their own struggles directly.

Protecting Self-Image: Seeking help can be perceived as a sign of weakness by some individuals. They might be concerned about preserving a self-image of competence and self-sufficiency, so they use the "friend" as a buffer to avoid any potential negative impact on their self-esteem.

Emotional Avoidance: Addressing personal problems can be emotionally challenging, and some individuals may attempt to avoid facing their emotions or vulnerabilities by focusing on someone else's situation.

Difficulty Expressing Vulnerability: Admitting one's need for help or support requires being vulnerable, which can be uncomfortable for some people. Using a proxy allows them to indirectly explore their concerns while maintaining emotional distance.

Fear of Dependency: People may fear becoming overly reliant on others or being seen as burdensome. Asking for advice for a "friend" can be a way to explore their own issues while maintaining a sense of independence.

Lack of Self-Awareness: In some cases, individuals may not fully recognize their own emotional struggles or the need for help. By focusing on a "friend's" situation, they may indirectly gain insight into their own challenges.

It's important for counselors and psychologists to be attuned to proxy seeking behavior during counseling sessions. Encouraging open and non-judgmental communication can help create a safe space for clients to share their concerns honestly. Establishing a strong therapeutic alliance based on trust and empathy can also encourage clients to be more forthcoming about their own experiences.

When someone is reluctant to admit they need help, the counselor can use therapeutic techniques such as active listening, empathy, and gentle exploration of their concerns to help them feel understood and supported. Gradually, the client may feel more comfortable revealing their true needs and challenges, allowing for a deeper and more effective therapeutic process.

Proxy seeking can be a starting point for addressing deeper psychological issues and fostering personal growth and self-awareness. By creating a supportive and non-judgmental therapeutic environment, counselors can help clients feel more comfortable opening up about their struggles and working toward positive change.

Crying With Laughter

I am wondering what the exact physiological and psychological process are that makes you cry when you laugh too hard. When this happens to me, sometimes the laughter and good feeling actually turns into a feeling of sorrow and sadness and go from laughing hysterically (if I'm being tickled for example) to sorrowfully weeping. Why does this happen?

When we laugh intensely, it can trigger the activation of the parasympathetic nervous system, which is responsible for the body's "rest and digest" response. Laughter involves deep breathing, which can lead to an increase in oxygen intake. This, in turn, stimulates the parasympathetic nervous system, leading to a sense of relaxation and well-being.

During moments of intense laughter, the body may also experience an increase in arousal and heightened emotional responses. This can result in the activation of the body's "fight or flight" response, which is controlled by the sympathetic nervous system. When the parasympathetic and sympathetic nervous systems are both activated simultaneously, it can create a unique and intense physiological experience.

Psychological Process: The transition from laughter to feelings of sorrow and sadness can be attributed to several psychological factors:

Catharsis: Intense emotions, such as laughter, can sometimes lead to a release of pent-up emotions. Laughing can serve as a form of catharsis, allowing individuals to release stress, tension, or even emotions that have been suppressed.

Emotional Vulnerability: When laughter reaches an extreme level, it can create a state of emotional vulnerability. In this heightened emotional state, individuals may be more receptive to accessing deeper emotions, including feelings of sorrow or sadness.

Complex Emotional Responses: Human emotions are complex, and they can often coexist or rapidly shift from one to another. What may start as pure joy and laughter can trigger thoughts or memories associated with sadness or grief, leading to a change in emotional state.

Social Context: The social environment can also influence emotional experiences. For example, if laughter occurs in a situation where individuals feel safe, supported, or emotionally connected to others, it may enhance the likelihood of experiencing a full range of emotions.

Tickling and Vulnerability: In situations where laughter is induced by tickling, the physical sensations of being tickled may induce a sense of vulnerability. This vulnerability can be accompanied by a release of emotions, including laughter and tears.

It's important to note that these physiological and psychological processes can vary from person to person and may be influenced by individual differences, personality traits, past experiences, and the specific context in which the laughter occurs.

The experience of transitioning from laughter to feelings of sorrow and sadness is a unique aspect of human emotions and highlights the interconnectedness of our emotional experiences. Emotions are multifaceted, and laughter and tears can often be expressions of complex emotional responses.

Remembering Names

I have a terrible memory for remembering names. Is there anything I can do to improve this using tips and research findings from psychology?

Here are some practical tips and insights from cognitive psychology to help improve your memory for remembering names:

Pay Attention and Be Present: One of the most crucial factors in remembering names is to pay close attention when you're introduced to someone. Often, forgetting a name happens because we're not fully present during the introduction. Make a conscious effort to focus on the person and their name.

Repeat and Reinforce: After you've been introduced, use the person's name in the conversation. For example, "Nice to meet you, Sarah." This repetition helps reinforce the memory trace. Repetition is a powerful tool for memory enhancement.

Use Visual Imagery: Try to create a mental image that connects the person's name with a distinctive visual cue. For example, if you meet someone named "Rose," imagine them holding a rose. Associating a name with a visual image can make it easier to recall.

Chunking: If the name is complex or long, break it down into smaller chunks.

For instance, if the name is "Jonathan," you can think of "John" and "Nathan." This technique can make it easier for your brain to process and remember.

Association: Connect the person's name with something you already know or a familiar person. For example, if the person has the same name as a friend or celebrity, associate the two in your mind.

Use the Name Immediately: In conversations, try to use the person's name naturally. "What do you think, David?" Using the name shortly after learning it helps reinforce memory.

Mindful Repetition: Spend a few minutes at the end of the day recalling the names of people you met. This mindful repetition can solidify memory storage.

Contextualize: If you meet someone in a specific context (at a party, in a class, at work), mentally associate their name with that context. This can provide a helpful retrieval cue later.

Active Listening: When people introduce themselves, they may also share something about themselves. Pay attention to these details as they can help you remember their names later.

Mnemonic Devices: Create mnemonic devices or memory aids to help remember names. These can be rhymes, alliterations, or acronyms based on the person's name.

Practice and Patience: Improving memory takes practice. Be patient with yourself and consistently apply these techniques.

Remember that memory improvement is a gradual process, and not all techniques may work equally well for everyone. Experiment with these strategies to find what works best for you. Over time, with consistent effort, you'll likely notice improvement in your ability to remember names.

Socially Awkward

Something I've noticed getting progressively worse over time is my social interaction with people. I used to be a happy-go-lucky always giddy class clown back in my grade-school days, more specifically middle school and about half of high school. I'm 21 now, and in college. So here it is: I feel GREATLY uncomfortable around people I don't know. I have a small group of close friends that I am perfectly fine with, but with everyone else it feels really different. I'll sit there quietly while everyone else is talking amongst each other. But here is my biggest issue. The conversations are usually about something I really don't have any say in. How am I supposed to respond to a conversation that's about nothing I know of, or about a situation in which I was not present to witness? So I just sit there, and people think I'm just unfriendly or shy, when I really just have nothing to say!

Another factor to this situation is the fact that I really can't talk all that well. I mean, I CAN talk, its just whenever I attempt to respond to someone or start a conversation, I really don't know how to start/say whatever it is I was going to say. I sometimes slur my words, forget a detail and go back in the conversation (usually a lot, and it feels really embarrassing when I do). That's pretty much it. It's a lot worse than it might sound. It really kills my social self-esteem when I can't even get my words right. Any ideas as to what I can do to help myself? Or at least to give it a name?

I'm sorry to hear that you've been experiencing difficulties with social interaction, and I want you to know that you're not alone in feeling this way. It's not uncommon for social dynamics to change as we go through different stages of life, and it's essential to address these challenges with empathy and understanding.

The difficulties you described in social situations may be attributed to a few factors, and it's possible that they are interconnected. Let's break them down:

Social Anxiety: Feeling uncomfortable around people you don't know and experiencing difficulty in conversations may be signs of social anxiety. Social anxiety is a common condition where individuals feel self-conscious, anxious, or inadequate in social settings. This can lead to avoidance of social situations or staying quiet to avoid drawing attention to oneself.

Communication Challenges: The difficulty in finding the right words or slurring speech may be related to communication issues such as social communication disorder or speech impediments. These challenges can make it harder to engage in conversations and may contribute to feelings of self-consciousness and embarrassment.

Low Self-Esteem: Struggling in social interactions and feeling like you can't express yourself effectively can have a negative impact on self-esteem. It's important to recognize that communication challenges do not define your worth, but they can impact your confidence in social settings.

Given these factors, it might be beneficial to consider seeking support to address your social difficulties. Here are some suggestions:

Therapy or Counseling: Consider speaking with a therapist or counselor who specializes in social anxiety or communication challenges. They can provide strategies to manage anxiety, improve communication skills, and work on building self-esteem.

Speech Therapy: If communication challenges are a significant concern, speech therapy can help improve speech fluency and clarity.

Social Skills Training: Social skills training can be beneficial in learning how to navigate social situations, engage in conversations, and respond to various topics.

Support Groups: Joining support groups or social clubs can provide a safe space to practice social interactions and meet others who may have similar experiences.

Practice and Patience: Improving social skills takes time and practice. Be patient with yourself and recognize that it's okay to feel uncomfortable at times. With support and effort, you can make progress.

It's important to remember that you are not alone, and seeking help is a brave and positive step towards personal growth and improvement. There is no need to label yourself with a specific name for your challenges, as what matters most is taking steps to address and overcome them. You deserve to feel comfortable and confident in social situations, and with the right support, it is possible to achieve that.

Why Do We Daydream

What does psychology have to say about the purpose of daydreaming?

Here are some insights into the phenomenon of daydreaming from the perspective of psychology, including its potential functions and underlying mechanisms.

Daydreaming is a cognitive phenomenon characterized by spontaneous shifts of attention away from the external environment to internal thoughts, fantasies, or imagined scenarios. While daydreaming might seem like a distraction from reality, it serves several important psychological functions:

Problem Solving and Creativity: Daydreaming allows the mind to engage in free-form thinking and explore creative ideas. When the mind wanders, it can make novel connections between different concepts, leading to creative insights and problem-solving.

Emotion Regulation: Daydreaming can serve as a form of emotional self-regulation. When experiencing stress, boredom, or negative emotions, daydreaming can provide an escape or a way to process emotions and reduce psychological distress.

Planning and Goal Setting: Daydreaming can involve envisioning future scenarios and imagining potential outcomes. This can aid in setting goals, creating plans, and envisioning the steps needed to achieve them.

Memory Consolidation: Some research suggests that daydreaming plays a role in consolidating and integrating information from recent experiences, helping to organize memories and improve overall learning.

Social Simulation: Daydreaming can involve imagining social interactions and scenarios, which can help individuals practice social skills, empathy, and perspective-taking.

Entertainment and Enjoyment: Engaging in positive daydreams can be pleasurable and entertaining, providing a mental break from routine tasks and enhancing overall well-being.

Self-Reflection: Daydreaming allows individuals to engage in self-reflection and introspection, helping them understand their own thoughts, desires, and personal goals.

Underlying Mechanisms:

Daydreaming is facilitated by the brain's "default mode network" (DMN), a network of brain regions that becomes active when we are not focused on external tasks. The DMN is associated with self-referential thinking, introspection, and mental time travel. When the mind is not occupied by external demands, the DMN becomes more active, leading to daydreaming.

It's important to note that daydreaming exists on a continuum, ranging from simple fleeting thoughts to more elaborate and immersive mental experiences. The content of daydreams can vary widely based on individual interests, experiences, and cognitive processes.

While daydreaming has many potential benefits, excessive or unfocused daydreaming can sometimes interfere with daily tasks and responsibilities. Striking a balance between productive daydreaming and maintaining focus on important tasks is key for overall cognitive functioning and well-being.

In summary then, daydreaming is a natural and multifaceted cognitive process that serves various functions, including problem-solving, emotional regulation, creativity, planning, and memory consolidation. It provides a window into the mind's capacity for imagination, introspection, and mental exploration.

Related Information on The All About Psychology Website

www.all-about-psychology.com/what-is-daydreaming.html

Great article based on research that found that mind-wandering seems to happen when parts of the brain fall asleep while most of it remains awake.

www.all-about-psychology.com/maladaptive-daydreaming.html

The compulsive, complex fantasy disorder that dominates some people's daily lives. Fascinating article by Giulia Poerio, Associate lecturer, University of Sussex.

Availability Heuristic

I would be really grateful if someone could give me a simple example of the availability heuristic. Thank you.

The availability heuristic is a cognitive bias that leads people to rely on the ease with which examples come to mind when making judgments about the probability of events. Essentially, if something is easily brought to mind, it's often perceived as being more likely to occur. This mental shortcut can sometimes lead to errors in judgment, as the ease of recall may not accurately reflect the true likelihood of an event.

Here's a simple example of the availability heuristic:

Imagine you're planning a beach vacation, and you've heard news reports about shark attacks in the past few months. Even though shark attacks are relatively rare events, the vividness and media coverage of these incidents make them stand out in your mind. As a result, you might become overly concerned about the possibility of a shark attack during your vacation.

In this scenario, the availability heuristic is at play. The ease with which you can recall news stories about shark attacks makes them seem more prevalent and likely than they actually are. As a result, you might make decisions based on this exaggerated perception of risk, such as avoiding swimming in the ocean altogether or feeling anxious throughout your vacation.

The availability heuristic can influence various areas of decision making, such as evaluating risks, estimating probabilities, and forming opinions. It's important to recognize that the availability heuristic can lead to biases when making judgments, as events that are more memorable or easily recalled may not accurately represent the overall likelihood of those events occurring.

To mitigate the effects of the availability heuristic, individuals can:

1. Seek out more comprehensive and accurate information rather than relying solely on easily recalled examples.

2. Consider a broader range of experiences and data before making judgments.

3.Recognize that vivid or recent examples may not necessarily reflect the true frequency or probability of events.

By being mindful of the availability heuristic and its potential impact on decision making, individuals can make more informed and rational choices based on a more balanced understanding of the actual probabilities involved.

Related Information on The All About Psychology Website

www.all-about-psychology.com/behavioral-economics.html

Person Centered Therapy

What are the main principles of Carl Rogers' person centered therapy?

Carl Rogers' person-centered therapy, also known as client-centered therapy is rooted in humanistic psychology and emphasizes the importance of creating a supportive and empathetic therapeutic environment. Here are the key principles:

Unconditional Positive Regard: Rogers believed in providing clients with genuine acceptance and respect, regardless of their thoughts, feelings, or behaviors. Therapists practicing person-centered therapy offer unconditional positive regard, creating a nonjudgmental and safe space where clients can freely express themselves without fear of criticism or rejection.

Empathy: Empathy is a cornerstone of person-centered therapy. Therapists actively listen and seek to understand the client's perspective and emotions. Through empathy, therapists connect deeply with clients and demonstrate that they genuinely care about the client's experiences and feelings.

Congruence (Genuineness): Therapists in person-centered therapy aim to be authentic and transparent in their interactions with clients. They openly share their own feelings and reactions, fostering a sense of genuine and honest communication. This congruence helps build trust and rapport between the therapist and client.

Focus on the "Here and Now": Person-centered therapy primarily focuses on the client's present experiences, thoughts, and feelings. The therapist helps the client explore their current challenges, emotions, and self-perceptions to gain insight into their inner world and facilitate personal growth.

Non-Directive Approach: Person-centered therapy is non-directive, meaning that the therapist does not provide advice, solutions, or interpretations. Instead, therapists help clients find their own insights and solutions by encouraging self-exploration and self-discovery.

Client as the Expert: In this approach, the client is considered the expert on their own life. The therapist trusts that clients have the capacity to understand themselves and make positive changes. The therapist's role is to facilitate the client's self-exploration and self-actualization.

Personal Growth and Self-Actualization: Person-centered therapy aims to help clients reach their full potential and achieve self-actualization—a state of personal fulfillment and growth. By providing an accepting and empathetic environment, therapists support clients in their journey toward becoming their authentic selves.

Minimal Therapist Interpretation: Unlike some other therapeutic approaches, person-centered therapy avoids heavy interpretations or analysis by the therapist. Instead, the focus is on the client's self-discovery and self-awareness.

Promotion of Autonomy: Person-centered therapy empowers clients to take ownership of their therapeutic process. Therapists encourage clients to make choices, set goals, and take steps toward personal growth based on their own values and preferences.

In summary, Carl Rogers' person-centered therapy emphasizes the importance of creating a warm and supportive therapeutic relationship where clients feel understood, accepted, and empowered to explore their thoughts and emotions. The principles of empathy, unconditional positive regard, and congruence guide therapists in helping clients achieve personal growth and greater self-awareness.

Related Information on The All About Psychology Website

www.all-about-psychology.com/carl_rogers.html

Learn all about the life and work of Carl Rogers, a profoundly influential figure in the humanistic movement towards person centered theory and non-directive psychotherapy.

https://www.all-about-psychology.com/carl-rogers.html

Persons or Science? A Philosophical Question. Classic article by Carl Rogers.

Self Induced Amnesia

Is it possible to self induce amnesia?

Amnesia refers to a significant loss of memory that is typically caused by brain injury, trauma, medical conditions, or psychological factors. It is important to understand that amnesia is a complex neurological and psychological phenomenon, and it is not possible to intentionally induce amnesia in oneself through mere psychological efforts.

The human brain has intricate mechanisms for memory formation, storage, and retrieval. Amnesia can result from damage to brain structures involved in these processes, such as the hippocampus and other parts of the limbic system. In cases of amnesia caused by trauma or injury, the brain's normal functioning is disrupted, leading to memory deficits.

Attempting to self-induce amnesia through psychological means, such as meditation, hypnosis, or other techniques, is not supported by scientific evidence and could potentially be harmful. These practices are not effective for erasing or altering memories in the same way that amnesia resulting from brain injury occurs.

It is also important to note that memory is a fundamental aspect of our identity and functioning. Losing memories can have significant psychological and emotional consequences, and intentionally trying to induce amnesia could lead to distress and confusion.

If you are seeking to manage distressing memories or experiences, it is recommended to consult with a qualified mental health professional. Therapists who specialize in trauma-focused therapies, such as Eye Movement Desensitization and Reprocessing (EMDR) or cognitive-behavioral therapy (CBT), can help individuals process and cope with difficult memories in a safe and therapeutic manner.

Self-induced amnesia is not a viable or recommended approach to dealing with psychological distress or unwanted memories. Seeking professional guidance and evidence-based therapeutic interventions is a more appropriate and effective way to address memory-related concerns.

Related Information on The All About Psychology Website

www.all-about-psychology.com/real-life-cases-of-amnesia-that-are-stranger-than-fiction.html

Fascinating article by psychologist, award-winning writer and best selling author Dr. Christian Jarrett.

Strange Irrational Fears

I have a nearly overpowering fear of abandoned/deserted structures and landmarks, i.e., malls, amusement parks, drive-in movie screens, etc. The only thing I can attribute this to is a dream I had when I was a child where a giant movie-sized gorilla appeared out of this blank drive-in screen and tried to snatch me out of my grandmother's house (about age 6). Several years ago I visited a mall I had shopped at frequently in Nashville TN, years before only to find it completely deserted except for a Chik-Fil-A and a Macy's. My husband was with me or I probably would've had to be committed. I could not get out of there fast enough, it looked like a good place for a mass murder (if anybody except for us had been there).

I can't explain the feeling I had, my whole body went numb, I had the most awful anxiety I have ever had and terrible feelings of dread came over my body in waves. I was attached at the hip to my husband for several hours. I cannot even pass an old drive-in screen (or a functional one in the daylight for that matter) without shutting my eyes or if I'm driving turning my head the other way for several miles until I am sure I'm past it. The same feelings of dread overwhelm me during this.

Today, I came across (by accident) a website about abandoned amusement parks, complete with pictures and I nearly became unglued with the same feelings I described, numbness to my whole body, smothering anxiety and complete terror. I actually considered leaving work to be with my husband. The odd thing is if I see a website like this, it's almost like seeing a dead body - you look, then you look away in horror, but you want to look again. Why do I have this paralyzing fear? What is wrong with me? I am very normal by societal standards in every other way. Here's hoping you can shed some light on this. Thank you very much.

I want to begin by acknowledging the distress and discomfort that your fear of abandoned structures and landmarks, as well as the specific experiences you've described, have caused you. It's important to recognize that fears and anxieties, even when they seem unusual or irrational, are valid and real experiences for the individuals who face them.

The fear you've described appears to be a specific phobia, which is an intense and irrational fear of a particular situation, object, or place. In your case, your fear seems to be related to abandoned or deserted structures and landmarks, which trigger significant anxiety and distress. Phobias can develop due to a combination of factors, including genetics, personal experiences, and learned responses. Here are a few points to consider:

Early Childhood Experience: You mentioned a dream you had as a child involving a giant gorilla and a drive-in screen. Early childhood experiences, even dream-related ones, can have a lasting impact on our emotions and perceptions. Traumatic or distressing events, even if they occurred during a dream, can sometimes contribute to the development of phobias.

Learned Responses: Over time, your mind may have associated feelings of anxiety, dread, and discomfort with abandoned or deserted places due to that childhood experience. Additionally, the intense anxiety you felt during the visit to the deserted mall might have reinforced these associations.

Fear Generalization: Once a fear or phobia develops, it can sometimes generalize to other similar situations or stimuli. This might explain why you experience anxiety not only around deserted structures you encountered in person but also when viewing images of abandoned places online.

Protective Instinct: The intense anxiety you experience may be connected to a primal protective instinct. Your mind might be associating these settings with potential danger or harm, leading to heightened physiological and emotional responses.

Empowerment through Understanding: It's important to remember that your fear doesn't define your overall well-being or normalcy. Phobias are relatively common and can be addressed with the right strategies and support. Seeking professional help from a therapist who specializes in anxiety and phobias can provide you with effective tools and techniques to manage and overcome your fear.

Cognitive-behavioral therapy (CBT) is often used to treat phobias. It can help you understand the thought patterns and behaviors contributing to your fear and work towards changing them. Exposure therapy, a specific type of CBT, gradually exposes you to the feared situations in a controlled and safe manner, helping you reduce anxiety over time.

Remember, you're not alone in your experience, and seeking help is a proactive step towards addressing and managing your fear. Your ability to reach out and seek understanding is a testament to your strength. It's okay to ask for support, and with the right guidance, you can work towards finding relief from this paralyzing fear.

Emotional Detachment

What causes emotional detachment?

Emotional detachment, often referred to as emotional numbness or emotional disconnection, is a complex psychological phenomenon that can have various underlying causes. It involves a reduced or limited emotional response to situations or relationships that would typically evoke feelings.

Below are some of the factors that can contribute to emotional detachment:

Trauma and Post-Traumatic Stress: Individuals who have experienced significant trauma, such as physical or emotional abuse, may develop emotional detachment as a coping mechanism. This detachment serves as a way to protect oneself from overwhelming emotions associated with traumatic experiences.

Depression: Severe depression can lead to emotional numbness and detachment. People with depression may feel a general lack of interest or pleasure in activities they used to enjoy, and this can extend to emotional experiences as well.

Anxiety Disorders: Certain anxiety disorders, particularly those characterized by chronic stress or excessive worry, can lead to emotional detachment. The constant state of heightened alertness and worry may result in emotional numbing as a way to manage overwhelming feelings.

Grief and Loss: After experiencing a significant loss, such as the death of a loved one or a major life change, some individuals may detach emotionally as a defense mechanism to cope with the pain of grief.

Personality Disorders: Certain personality disorders, such as borderline personality disorder, can be associated with difficulties in regulating emotions. Emotional detachment may be a way to manage intense emotional experiences.

Substance Abuse: Substance abuse and addiction can alter brain chemistry and interfere with emotional processing, leading to emotional detachment.

Chronic Stress: Prolonged exposure to high levels of stress, especially when accompanied by a lack of effective coping strategies, can contribute to emotional detachment as a way to manage overwhelming feelings.

Dissociation: Some individuals may experience dissociation, a psychological defense mechanism that involves disconnecting from one's thoughts, feelings, and surroundings. This can result in emotional detachment.

Unresolved Past Experiences: Unresolved emotional conflicts or experiences from the past may contribute to emotional detachment in the present.

Medical Conditions: Certain medical conditions that affect brain function, such as neurological disorders or brain injuries, can impact emotional processing and lead to detachment.

It's important to note that emotional detachment can vary in severity and may manifest differently in different individuals. If you or someone you know is experiencing emotional detachment and it is causing distress or interfering with daily functioning, seeking the guidance of a qualified mental health professional is recommended. Therapists can provide assessment, support, and appropriate interventions to address the underlying causes and work toward emotional well-being.

The Psychology of Hoarding

My mom likes to keep all old, unused, broken or spoilt things. My house is full of empty bottles, can, container, newspapers, flyers, old clothes, old furniture & electrical appliances, etc. Please tell me how can I change her strange habit and get rid of all this stuff. I Have tried to explain to her many times but she is too stubborn to listen and never tries to understand my feelings. Anybody have a solution to this problem? Thanks.

Addressing a loved one's hoarding tendencies or attachment to old and unused items can be a delicate and challenging situation. It's essential to approach this issue with empathy and understanding. Here are some steps to consider when trying to help your mom change her habit:

Open and Honest Communication: Start by having a calm and non-confrontational conversation with your mom. Express your concern for her well-being and the safety of the household due to the clutter. Use "I" statements to communicate your feelings, such as "I feel overwhelmed by the clutter, and it's affecting my peace of mind."

Listen Actively: Give your mom an opportunity to share her perspective. Ask her why she feels the need to keep these items. Understanding her motivations is essential to finding a solution that addresses her underlying needs.

Professional Guidance: Consider involving a mental health professional or counselor who specializes in hoarding behavior. They can provide an objective assessment and offer strategies for managing hoarding tendencies.

Small Steps: Encourage your mom to start small. Suggest tackling one area or category of items at a time, such as old newspapers or clothing. Setting achievable goals can make the process less overwhelming.

Support and Involvement: Offer your assistance in decluttering. Your mom may be more willing to part with items if she feels supported and not judged. Be patient and understanding during the process.

Donate or Recycle: Emphasize the positive impact of donating or recycling items that are no longer needed. Knowing that these items may benefit others can be a motivating factor for decluttering.

Safety and Functionality: Highlight the importance of safety and functionality in the home. Clutter can pose safety risks, and a more organized living space can enhance daily living.

Seeking Community Resources: Investigate local hoarding support groups or community resources. Connecting with others who have experienced similar challenges can provide valuable insights and encouragement.

Respect Boundaries: While encouraging change, respect your mom's boundaries and pace. Avoid pressuring her or making decisions about her belongings without her consent.

Maintenance Plan: Once progress is made, work together to establish a maintenance plan to prevent clutter from accumulating again. Regularly decluttering and organizing can help maintain a clutter-free environment.

Changing deeply ingrained habits, such as hoarding tendencies, can be a gradual process. Be patient, empathetic, and persistent in your efforts to support your mom.

Related Information on The All About Psychology Website

www.all-about-psychology.com/the-psychology-of-hoarding.html

Learn all about this complex and debilitating condition characterized by the persistent difficulty discarding or parting with possessions.

PSYOP Meaning

I'm doing some background research on psychological operations (PSYOP) and need a clear and concise definition of what PSYOP means. I would be super grateful for any suggestions. I'm also looking for information about the history of psychological operations and an example of a PSYOP. Many thanks for your time.

Good luck with your research, Psychological Operations is a fascinating topic. Hope the following information helps.

Definition of Psychological Operations (PSYOP):

Psychological operations, often abbreviated as PSYOP, are planned and deliberate efforts to influence the thoughts, emotions, attitudes, and behavior of specific target audiences. These operations use a variety of communication techniques and channels, such as propaganda, information warfare, and strategic messaging, to achieve specific objectives. PSYOP can be conducted by military or government agencies and are typically aimed at achieving strategic, political, or military goals by shaping perceptions and behavior.

History of Psychological Operations:

Psychological operations have a long history dating back to ancient civilizations, but they gained prominence during the 20th century, especially during times of war. Here are key historical points:

World War I: Psychological operations were informally used during WWI, with both sides disseminating propaganda to boost morale and demoralize the enemy.

World War II: PSYOP became more systematic during WWII, with dedicated units producing leaflets, radio broadcasts, and other media to influence enemy and occupied populations.

Korean War: The Korean War saw the use of PSYOP leaflets, loudspeakers, and radio broadcasts aimed at both enemy combatants and civilian populations.

Vietnam War: The Vietnam War witnessed extensive use of PSYOP, including leaflet drops, broadcasts, and the Chieu Hoi program, which aimed to encourage defection from the Viet Cong.

Cold War: Throughout the Cold War, PSYOP was a critical component of the ideological struggle between the United States and the Soviet Union, with both sides engaging in information warfare.

Modern Era: In contemporary conflicts, such as the Gulf War, Iraq War, and Afghanistan War, psychological operations have evolved to include digital media, social media, and internet-based propaganda.

Example of a PSYOP:

One notable example of a PSYOP is the "Operation Mincemeat" during World War II. In 1943, British intelligence orchestrated a deception operation to mislead Nazi Germany about the Allied invasion of Southern Europe (Operation Husky). They acquired the corpse of a deceased man, dressed him as a Royal Marine officer, and attached a briefcase to his wrist containing fake documents suggesting an imminent Allied invasion of Sardinia and Greece instead of Sicily, the actual target.

The corpse was released into the sea off the coast of Spain, where it washed ashore. Spanish authorities, who were sympathetic to the Axis but also neutral, shared the documents with the Germans. As a result, the Germans diverted their troops away from Sicily, and the Allied invasion of Sicily in 1943, codenamed Operation Husky, encountered less resistance.

Operation Mincemeat is a classic example of how psychological operations can be used to deceive and manipulate the enemy's perceptions and decision-making, ultimately achieving strategic objectives.

Maslow's Hierarchy of Needs

What are the 5 levels of Maslow hierarchy of needs?

Abraham Maslow's Hierarchy of Needs is a well-known psychological theory that describes human motivation and the hierarchical nature of human needs. It is often depicted as a pyramid (*although Maslow never used the image of a pyramid to help illustrate his theory*) with the most basic physiological needs forming the broad base and self-actualization at the pinnacle. According to Maslow, individuals typically progress through these levels sequentially, with each level serving as a foundation for the next. However, individuals may revisit lower levels if their higher-level needs are not met. The 5 levels of Maslow hierarchy of needs are as follows:

1. Physiological Needs: This is the foundational level of the hierarchy and includes the most basic human needs necessary for survival. It encompasses things like air, water, food, shelter, sleep, and clothing. Without these needs met, individuals cannot progress to higher levels of the hierarchy.

2. Safety Needs: Once physiological needs are reasonably satisfied, individuals seek safety and security. This level includes the need for physical safety, financial security, health, and protection from harm. People may seek stable employment, access to healthcare, and a safe living environment.

3. Love and Belongingness Needs: After the lower levels are met, individuals desire social connections and a sense of belonging. This includes the need for love, friendship, intimacy, and a sense of community. People seek relationships with family, friends, and romantic partners to fulfill these needs.

4. Esteem Needs: Once the lower levels are fulfilled, individuals strive for self-esteem and a positive self-image. This level encompasses both self-esteem (confidence, achievement, respect from others) and the need for esteem from others (recognition, status, appreciation). Achieving personal goals and receiving recognition become essential at this stage.

5. Self-Actualization: At the top of the hierarchy is self-actualization, which represents the realization of one's full potential and personal growth. This level involves pursuing personal interests, self-discovery, creativity, and fulfilling one's unique capabilities. People at this stage are often driven by a desire for personal growth, self-fulfillment, and a deeper understanding of themselves and the world around them.

Maslow's Hierarchy of Needs has been influential in various fields, including psychology, education, and management, as it provides a framework for understanding human motivation and behavior and can inform strategies for personal development and well-being.

Related Information on The All About Psychology Website

www.all-about-psychology.com/do-you-have-a-self-actualised-personality.html

Excellent article by Dr. Christian Jarrett on the use of modern statistical methods to create a test of self-actualisation.

Color Psychology

How do colors affect mood, emotion, and psychological wellbeing?

Colors have a significant impact on human psychology and can evoke a wide range of emotions, moods, and feelings. Color psychology, explores how different colors can affect our mental and emotional states. While individual responses to colors can vary based on personal experiences and cultural factors, there are some general associations between colors and mood, emotion, and psychological wellbeing.

Red:

Red is often associated with strong emotions such as love, anger, and passion. It can create a sense of urgency or excitement. Red can increase heart rate and stimulate the senses. It may also enhance attention to detail but can be overwhelming in excess.

Blue:

Blue is linked to calmness, tranquility, and serenity. It can promote a sense of relaxation and reduce anxiety. Blue is often used in healthcare settings to create a soothing environment. It can also enhance concentration and focus.

Green:

Green is associated with nature, growth, and renewal. It can induce feelings of harmony, balance, and refreshment. Green is thought to reduce stress and promote a sense of well-being. It is often linked to environmental consciousness.

Yellow:

Yellow is linked to happiness, energy, and positivity. It can uplift spirits and create a cheerful atmosphere. Yellow is thought to stimulate mental activity and boost creativity. However, excessive yellow can be agitating for some individuals.

Purple:

Purple is associated with luxury, spirituality, and creativity. It can evoke a sense of mystery and introspection. Purple is often used to promote relaxation and balance. It may also encourage artistic and imaginative thinking.

Orange:

Orange is linked to enthusiasm, vitality, and warmth. It can create a sense of excitement and motivation. Orange is believed to stimulate social interaction and boost energy levels. It may also increase appetite.

Pink:

Pink is associated with love, tenderness, and nurturing. It can induce feelings of calmness and affection. Pink is often used to create a soothing and gentle atmosphere. It can reduce aggression and promote a sense of safety.

It's important to recognise that individual responses to colors can vary, and cultural factors play a significant role in color associations. Additionally, personal experiences and context can influence how colors affect mood and psychological wellbeing. For example, a color that has positive connotations in one culture may have different meanings in another.

In design, marketing, and therapeutic settings, understanding the psychological impact of colors is essential. Using colors strategically can influence people's emotions and behaviors, whether it's creating a calming environment in a healthcare facility, using vibrant colors in advertising to evoke excitement, or selecting soothing hues for interior design to enhance relaxation and comfort.

Related Information on The All About Psychology Website

www.all-about-psychology.com/the-hidden-meanings-behind-colors-a-guide-to-color-psychology.html

www.all-about-psychology.com/how-colors-affect-mood.html

How to Start a Conversation

Does anybody have any tips on how to effectively start a conversation?

Starting a conversation effectively can be a valuable skill in various social and professional situations. Here are some tips on how to initiate conversations:

Smile and Make Eye Contact: A warm smile and friendly eye contact can signal approachability and set a positive tone for the conversation.

Use Open Body Language: Keep your body language relaxed and open. Avoid crossing your arms or appearing tense, as this can be off-putting.

Begin with a Greeting: Start with a simple greeting like "Hello," "Hi," or "Hey." Use the person's name if you know it, as it adds a personal touch.

Offer a Compliment or Observation: Compliments or observations about the environment or situation can be excellent conversation starters. For example, you could say, "I love the artwork in this room," or "The weather today is fantastic."

Ask Open-Ended Questions: Open-ended questions encourage the other person to share more about themselves and their thoughts. Instead of asking,

"Did you have a good weekend?" you could ask, "What did you do over the weekend?" This invites a more detailed response.

Show Genuine Interest: Pay attention to the other person's responses and show genuine interest in what they are saying. Nodding, making affirmative sounds (like "I see," or "That's interesting"), and maintaining good eye contact convey your attentiveness.

Share About Yourself: After asking a question, share a bit about yourself related to the topic. This reciprocation can help build rapport and keep the conversation balanced.

Listen Actively: Effective conversation involves active listening. Focus on what the other person is saying rather than thinking about your response. Ask follow-up questions to demonstrate your engagement.

Avoid Controversial Topics: When starting a conversation with someone you don't know well, it's generally best to steer clear of sensitive or controversial topics like politics or personal issues. Stick to neutral subjects.

Find Common Ground: Look for shared interests or experiences that can serve as a foundation for the conversation. Common ground helps establish a connection.

Use Mirroring: Subtly mirroring the other person's body language and speech patterns can create a sense of rapport. Be cautious not to overdo it.

Be Mindful of Personal Space: Respect personal space and avoid standing or sitting too close to someone you've just met. Give them room to feel comfortable.

Stay Positive: Maintain a positive and friendly tone throughout the conversation. Positivity is contagious and can make interactions more enjoyable.

Exit Gracefully: When you sense the conversation has reached a natural conclusion, express gratitude and exit gracefully. You might say, "It was lovely talking to you. Enjoy the rest of your day!"

Practice: Like any skill, starting conversations improves with practice. Challenge yourself to initiate conversations in various settings to build confidence.

Not every conversation will lead to a deep connection, and that's okay. The goal is to create a positive and engaging interaction that leaves both you and the other person feeling valued and heard.

Slip of the Tongue

My mom continues to occasionally call my spouse (and me) by the wrong name, generally the name of another friend or relative. Example: Joey...I mean bobby... My wife believes this is on purpose and is upset that I do not confront my mom on this issue. My wife also believes that she, me and anyone the slip happens to, occurs because they are really not liked by my mom.

This has been going on for least 25 years and is not isolated to me or my wife, but also her other children and grandchildren as well. I contend that there is no malice and that it is not being done on purpose and we should, therefore, just ignore it. Any thoughts?

The situation you describe can be challenging, and it's understandable that both you and your wife have different perspectives on it. The following information might help.

Possible Reasons for the Name Mix-Ups:

Cognitive Load: Sometimes, when people are stressed or have a lot on their minds, they might inadvertently mix up names. This can happen even when they care deeply about the people involved.

Verbal Slip: Language is complex, and verbal slips, including mixing up names, can occur for various reasons. These slips are not necessarily reflective of feelings toward the individuals involved.

Habit: If your mom has been doing this for a long time, it could have become a habit. Habits can be challenging to break, even if they are not intentional.

Addressing the Issue:

Empathetic Communication: It might be helpful for you and your wife to have an open and empathetic conversation with your mom about this issue. Express your feelings and concerns while emphasizing that you want to understand her perspective as well. Approach the conversation with the assumption that it's not intentional and that you're seeking a solution together.

Memory Support: If memory decline is a concern, encourage your mom to consider memory-enhancing strategies, such as puzzles, games, or memory exercises. You can frame this as a proactive approach to maintaining cognitive health.

Seek Professional Guidance: If the issue persists or escalates, and if it causes significant distress within your family, it may be worthwhile to consult a family therapist or counselor. They can provide guidance on effective communication and help navigate family dynamics.

Choose Your Battles: It's important to consider whether this issue is worth confronting. If it's causing undue stress and tension within your family, addressing it is important. However, if it's a minor issue that doesn't significantly impact your relationships, it might be worth letting go.

Model Understanding: Demonstrate understanding and patience when these mix-ups occur. If your mom sees that you and your wife are not overly bothered by it, she may become less self-conscious about the slips.

It's quite possible that the mix-ups are unintentional, and addressing the issue through open communication and support may help find a resolution that works for everyone.

Birth Order

Does birth order affect your personality?

The question of whether birth order affects personality has been a topic of interest and debate in psychology for many years. For example, in the 1930's Alfred Adler, renowned for coining the phrase *'inferiority complex'*, wrote widely on birth order and its effect on personality. His work in this area was driven by his firm belief that *"every difficulty of development is caused by rivalry and lack of cooperation in the family"*.

Birth order refers to the position of a child in a family concerning their siblings (e.g., firstborn, middle child, youngest), and it has been suggested that the role and experiences associated with birth order can influence personality development. Here are some key points on this topic:

Birth Order Theory:

Firstborns: According to birth order theories, firstborn children are often seen as responsible, reliable, and achievement-oriented. They tend to be natural leaders and may exhibit perfectionist tendencies. They often enjoy the attention and approval of their parents.

Middle Children: Middle children are thought to be more flexible, diplomatic, and sociable. They often develop strong negotiation and peacemaking skills. Middle children may seek attention by standing out in their own way.

Youngest Children: Youngest children are often seen as outgoing, charming, and creative. They may be more free-spirited and less concerned with rules and structure. Youngest children may use humor to gain attention.

Sibling Dynamics:

The specific influence of birth order on personality can be influenced by various factors, including family size, age differences between siblings, and individual family dynamics.

Siblings' relationships, such as rivalry, cooperation, or mentoring, can shape personality development.

Research Findings:

While some studies have reported correlations between birth order and personality traits, the effects tend to be modest. This means that while birth order may play a role, it is just one of many factors that shape personality. Research in this area has yielded mixed results, and there is no consensus among psychologists on the extent to which birth order directly determines personality.

Parenting Styles and Expectations:

Parenting styles and expectations can differ for each child based on their birth order. Firstborn children, for example, may experience more pressure to excel, while youngest children might benefit from more relaxed parenting. These differing parental approaches can contribute to variations in personality development.

Individual Differences:

It's important to recognize that individual differences play a significant role in personality development. Factors such as genetics, life experiences, cultural influences, and personal interests all contribute to shaping an individual's personality.

Modern Perspectives:

Contemporary psychology tends to emphasize the importance of a range of factors beyond birth order in understanding personality, such as genetics, early attachment experiences, and environmental influences.

Emotional Intelligence

What Is the Meaning of Emotional Intelligence?

Emotional Intelligence (EI), often referred to as Emotional Quotient (EQ), is a concept in psychology that refers to an individual's ability to recognize, understand, manage, and effectively use their own emotions and the emotions of others in various social and interpersonal situations. It encompasses a range of skills and qualities that contribute to emotional well-being, effective communication, and successful relationships. Here's a breakdown of the meaning and components of emotional intelligence:

1. Self-Awareness: This is the foundational component of emotional intelligence. It involves recognizing and understanding your own emotions, including being able to identify and label them accurately. Self-aware individuals can pinpoint how they feel in specific situations and why they feel that way.

2. Self-Regulation: Self-regulation involves the ability to manage and control your emotions effectively. This means being able to respond to emotional triggers in a balanced and constructive manner rather than reacting impulsively. It also involves managing stress and maintaining emotional composure.

3. Empathy: Empathy is the capacity to understand and share the feelings and perspectives of others. It involves being attuned to the emotions of those around you and demonstrating empathy through active listening and compassionate responses.

4. Social Skills: Effective social skills are another crucial aspect of emotional intelligence. This includes the ability to navigate social situations, build and maintain relationships, and communicate clearly and persuasively. It also involves conflict resolution and cooperation.

5. Motivation: Motivation in the context of emotional intelligence refers to a strong intrinsic drive to achieve personal and professional goals. It involves the ability to persevere in the face of challenges, maintain a positive outlook, and channel emotions in a way that promotes personal growth and achievement.

6. Recognizing Emotions in Others: Part of emotional intelligence is being able to accurately perceive and understand the emotions of others. This skill allows individuals to respond empathetically and effectively in social interactions.

7. Emotional Management: Emotional intelligence encompasses the capacity to handle other people's emotions sensitively. This involves providing support, understanding, and constructive feedback when necessary.

Importance of Emotional Intelligence:

Enhanced Relationships: High emotional intelligence fosters healthier and more rewarding relationships, as individuals can understand, communicate with, and support others effectively.

Effective Leadership: Leaders with high EI often excel in motivating and inspiring their teams. They can handle conflicts and stress while maintaining a positive work environment.

Personal Well-Being: People with well-developed emotional intelligence tend to experience lower levels of stress, better mental health, and improved overall well-being.

Career Success: Emotional intelligence is highly valued in the workplace. It can lead to better job performance, effective teamwork, and career advancement.

Conflict Resolution: Individuals with strong EI can navigate conflicts more constructively and find resolutions that benefit all parties involved.

Emotional intelligence is a multifaceted concept that encompasses a range of skills related to understanding and managing emotions, both in oneself and in others. Developing emotional intelligence can lead to more fulfilling relationships, increased personal well-being, and enhanced success in various aspects of life, including career and leadership roles.

Character Vs. Personality

What does psychology have to say about the difference between character and personality?

The concepts of "character" and "personality" are often used interchangeably, but within the field of psychology, they can have distinct meanings. Understanding the difference between character and personality can provide insights into how individuals' behavior, values, and ethics are shaped. Here's a breakdown of these two terms:

Personality:

Definition: Personality refers to a set of enduring traits, patterns of thoughts, feelings, and behaviors that are relatively consistent over time and across different situations. It encompasses an individual's temperament, emotional responses, cognitive style, and behavioral tendencies.

Nature: Personality traits are believed to have a significant genetic component and are relatively stable throughout a person's life. They are shaped by a combination of genetics, early experiences, and socialization.

Example: A person with a "conscientious" personality trait tends to be organized, reliable, and detail-oriented. This trait is consistent across various situations and over time, reflecting their general disposition.

Character:

Definition: Character refers to an individual's moral and ethical values, as well as their sense of right and wrong. It involves qualities such as integrity, honesty, empathy, and responsibility.

Nature: Character is shaped by an individual's upbringing, cultural influences, moral teachings, and personal choices. It reflects one's adherence to moral principles and their ability to act ethically.

Example: A person with a strong character might be known for their honesty and integrity. They consistently tell the truth and uphold ethical standards in both their personal and professional life.

Key Differences:

Consistency: Personality traits are relatively stable and consistent over time, while character relates to an individual's moral values and ethical choices.

Focus: Personality is more concerned with describing an individual's typical patterns of behavior and emotional responses, whereas character emphasizes moral values and ethical principles.

Development: Personality traits are believed to have a significant genetic component and are shaped by early experiences, while character is molded through moral teachings, cultural influences, and personal decisions.

Illustrating the Difference:

Consider an example involving two individuals:

Person A: This person has a personality characterized by introversion, meaning they tend to be reserved, reflective, and prefer solitary activities. This personality trait is consistent across various situations.

Person B: Person B, on the other hand, possesses a strong character marked by honesty and integrity. They are known for their ethical behavior and their commitment to telling the truth, even when faced with challenging situations.

In this example, Person A's introverted personality trait describes their typical behavioral patterns, while Person B's strong character reflects their moral values and commitment to honesty. Person A's introversion may remain relatively stable over time, while Person B's character is shaped by their moral development and ethical choices.

While personality and character are related aspects of an individual's psychological makeup, they focus on different dimensions of human behavior. Personality encompasses enduring traits and behavioral patterns, while character relates to an individual's moral values and ethical principles. Both contribute to shaping an individual's identity and how they interact with the world.

Related Information on The All About Psychology Website

www.all-about-psychology.com/personality-psychology.html

Why We Love Superheroes

Why do so many people love superheroes?

Superheroes offer a rich tapestry of themes and emotions that continue to captivate audiences of all ages. As such, the fascination with superheroes is a complex and multifaceted phenomenon that can be explained by a combination of psychological, social, and cultural factors. Here are a few of the reasons people love superheroes:

Escapism: Superhero stories often transport readers or viewers to fantastical worlds where the impossible becomes possible. This escapism provides a temporary break from the challenges and stressors of real life, offering a sense of wonder and adventure.

Identification and Aspiration: Superheroes are often portrayed as individuals with extraordinary abilities or qualities, and people can identify with them or aspire to be like them. This identification can be empowering, allowing individuals to imagine themselves as capable of overcoming obstacles and making a positive impact on the world.

Moral Clarity: Superhero stories typically feature clear distinctions between good and evil. They offer moral guidance and present ethical dilemmas that resonate with audiences. This moral clarity can be comforting and provide a sense of direction in a world that often feels morally ambiguous.

Empowerment: Superheroes are often ordinary individuals who gain extraordinary powers or skills. This theme of transformation and empowerment can inspire people to believe in their own potential for growth and change.

Community and Belonging: Fandoms around superheroes create a sense of community and belonging. People who share a passion for these characters and stories can connect with like-minded individuals, attend conventions, and engage in discussions about their favorite superheroes.

Catharsis: Superhero stories often involve intense action sequences and dramatic confrontations. These narratives can provide a cathartic release of tension and emotions, offering a safe and controlled way to experience excitement and adrenaline.

Hope and Optimism: Superheroes represent symbols of hope and optimism. They demonstrate that even in the face of overwhelming challenges, individuals can rise above and make a difference. This message can be particularly meaningful during difficult times.

Nostalgia: Many adults who grew up with superhero comics or TV shows have a deep sense of nostalgia for these characters. Revisiting these stories can evoke cherished memories and provide a sense of continuity with one's past.

Complexity and Depth: While superheroes often appear in straightforward, action-packed narratives, many modern portrayals have added depth and complexity to their characters. This complexity allows for more nuanced storytelling and appeals to a mature audience.

Visual Spectacle: The visual appeal of superhero films and comics, with their elaborate costumes, special effects, and epic battles, can be a major draw. The stunning visuals enhance the overall entertainment value.

Sense of Justice: Superheroes often seek justice and fight against injustice. This resonates with people's innate desire for fairness and a just society.

Continuity and Serialization: The serialized nature of superhero comics and movies keeps fans engaged over the long term. The ongoing storylines and character development provide a sense of anticipation and investment.

Fun Fact:

Psychologist, William Moulton Marston created, wrote and produced the Wonder Woman comic strip under the pseudonym Charles Moulton. Marston's work on lie detection is the reason why Wonder Woman has a Lasso of Truth! How cool is that?

Accident Proneness

I have a friend whose nickname is "hazard" because of his accident-proneness. Are some people naturally predisposed to accident-proneness?

While the term accident-proneness is commonly used, it lacks a precise scientific definition in psychology. That being said; however, there are several factors and psychological explanations that may shed light on why some people seem more accident-prone than others, namely:

Personality Traits:

Impulsivity: People who are impulsive tend to act without thinking through the consequences, which can lead to accidents.

Sensation-Seeking: Individuals with a high sensation-seeking personality may be more inclined to take risks, increasing their chances of accidents.

Carelessness: Some people may exhibit carelessness in their actions or behaviors, overlooking safety precautions.

Cognitive Factors: Cognitive factors, such as attention and perception, play a role in accident proneness. Individuals who struggle with attention deficits or perceptual difficulties may be more prone to accidents due to inattentiveness or misjudgment of situations.

Stress and Anxiety: High levels of stress and anxiety can impair concentration and decision-making, potentially leading to accidents. Anxious individuals may be more prone to nervousness and distraction, which can contribute to mishaps.

Environmental Factors: Sometimes, accident proneness can be attributed to the environment in which a person lives or works. Hazardous living conditions, poor workplace safety measures, or inadequate infrastructure can increase the risk of accidents for anyone exposed to these conditions.

Previous Experience: People who have experienced accidents or near-misses in the past may develop a heightened sensitivity to danger. Paradoxically, this heightened awareness could lead to increased anxiety and a greater likelihood of accidents.

Health Factors: Physical health conditions, such as certain medical conditions, medications, or sleep disorders, can affect a person's coordination, balance, and overall physical functioning, potentially increasing the likelihood of accidents.

Lifestyle Choices: Certain lifestyle choices, such as substance abuse or excessive alcohol consumption, can impair judgment and motor skills, increasing the risk of accidents.

Social and Cultural Factors: Cultural norms and social influences can affect risk-taking behavior. For example, some cultures may encourage riskier activities or discourage safety precautions.

The term "accident-prone" is somewhat stigmatizing, and accidents can happen to anyone. It's important to acknowledge, therefore, that factors contributing to accident proneness can be multifaceted and interconnected. As such, understanding accident proneness requires a comprehensive approach that takes individual characteristics, environments, and behavioral choices, into account.

Attachment Theory

What are the main principles of attachment theory?

Primarily associated with the work of British psychologist John Bowlby, attachment theory is an established framework that helps understand the bonds that form between children and their caregivers. It suggests that these early relationships significantly impact a child's emotional and social development. The main principles of attachment theory are:

Attachment is Innate: Attachment is considered an innate and biologically programmed behavior. Infants are born with the instinct to form attachments to ensure their survival and well-being.

Attachment Figures: Children form specific attachment bonds with one or a few primary caregivers, often their parents or guardians. These individuals are called attachment figures, and they play a central role in the child's life.

Secure Base: Attachment figures serve as a secure base from which the child can explore the world. When a child feels secure in their attachment, they are more likely to explore their environment, knowing they have a safe haven to return to when needed.

Internal Working Models: Children develop internal working models based on their early attachment experiences. These models serve as templates for future relationships and influence how individuals perceive and interact with others throughout their lives.

Attachment Styles: Attachment theory identifies different attachment styles based on the quality of the caregiver-child relationship:

Secure Attachment: Children with secure attachments feel safe exploring the world because they trust their caregiver will be responsive to their needs. They are more likely to develop positive relationships later in life.

Insecure-Avoidant Attachment: Children with this attachment style may not seek comfort from their caregiver and may handle distress independently. They may have difficulty trusting others in adulthood.

Insecure-Ambivalent/Resistant Attachment: Children with this attachment style may be anxious and uncertain about their caregiver's availability. They may have difficulty regulating their emotions and may become clingy or overly dependent in adulthood.

Disorganized Attachment: Some children display a disorganized attachment style, characterized by inconsistent behavior when seeking comfort. This style may result from inconsistent or traumatic caregiving experiences.

Critical Period: Attachment theory suggests that there is a critical period, typically during the first two years of life, during which the formation of attachments is most critical for healthy emotional development. However, attachments can be formed or modified throughout life.

Impact on Development: Early attachment experiences significantly impact a child's emotional, social, and cognitive development. Children with secure attachments tend to have better emotional regulation, social skills, and self-esteem.

Intergenerational Transmission: Attachment styles often get passed from one generation to the next. Parents who had secure attachments as children are more likely to provide secure attachments to their own children.

Therapeutic Applications: Attachment theory has influenced therapeutic approaches, such as attachment-based therapy and interventions aimed at helping individuals develop secure attachments and heal attachment-related wounds.

To summarize, attachment theory highlights the importance of early caregiver-child relationships in shaping a child's emotional and social development. Understanding attachment styles can provide insights into how individuals form and navigate relationships throughout their lives and guide interventions to support healthy attachment bonds.

Related Information on The All About Psychology Website

www.all-about-psychology.com/What-is-attachment.html

What Is Attachment and How Does It Affect Our Relationships? Informative article by Gery Karantzas, Associate professor in Social Psychology and Relationship Science at Deakin University.

What Is the Peak-End Rule

Could someone please explain what the 'The Peak-End Rule' is all about.

The Peak-End Rule is a psychological principle that suggests people tend to judge and remember past experiences, particularly emotional ones, based on the most intense (peak) moment of the experience and its ending. This rule was first proposed by the Nobel prize winning psychologist Daniel Kahneman and his colleagues in the late 1990s.

Here's a breakdown of the Peak-End Rule:

Peak Moment: This refers to the most emotionally intense part of an experience. It can be a positive or negative emotion, such as extreme joy, fear, or pain.

End Moment: This refers to how an experience concludes. It's the emotion or feeling you have at the very end of an event.

The central idea behind the Peak-End Rule is that people often don't remember an experience as a whole; instead, they rely heavily on the emotional intensity at its peak and how it concluded. This cognitive shortcut can influence how people evaluate and remember various events in their lives.

Here's an example to illustrate the Peak-End Rule:

Scenario: You decide to go to a theme park for a day of fun. During your visit, several things happen:

Morning: You wait in long lines for most rides, which is frustrating (negative).

Afternoon: You finally get on your favorite roller coaster, which is an exhilarating experience (positive peak).

Late Afternoon: It starts raining heavily, and you get drenched (negative).

Evening: The rain stops, and you enjoy a delicious meal (positive).

Night: While leaving, you lose your wallet (negative end).

When you reflect on your day at the theme park, the Peak-End Rule suggests that your overall memory and evaluation of the experience will be influenced by the most intense moments and how it ended:

You might remember the day as a mix of frustration (long lines), excitement (roller coaster), discomfort (rain), and distress (losing your wallet). The memory of the thrilling roller coaster ride and the frustration of losing your wallet will likely stand out the most. Despite some positive moments, the memory of losing your wallet as you left the park could leave you with a somewhat negative overall impression of the day.

In this example, the Peak-End Rule demonstrates how strong emotions, whether positive or negative, during the peak and ending moments of an experience can significantly shape our overall perception and memory of that experience.

The Peak-End Rule has important implications in various domains, including marketing, customer service, and healthcare. Businesses and service providers can enhance customer satisfaction by ensuring that the peak and ending moments of an interaction or service are positive. In healthcare, understanding the Peak-End Rule can help improve patient experiences and compliance with medical treatments.

Visual Imagery Benefits

Can creating visual images in your mind help you learn skills or enhance task performance?

Creating visual images in your mind, also known as visualization can help enhance learning, skill acquisition, and task performance. This concept has been extensively studied in psychology, particularly in the fields of cognitive psychology and sports psychology.

How visual imagery works and its impact on learning and performance:

Mental Rehearsal: Visual imagery involves mentally rehearsing or simulating an activity in your mind. It's like creating a mental "movie" of the task or skill you want to improve.

Activation of Brain Regions: When you engage in visual imagery, your brain activates many of the same regions as it would during actual physical practice of the task. This includes areas responsible for motor planning and execution.

Skill Enhancement: Visual imagery can enhance the development of motor skills and muscle memory. For example, athletes often use visualization techniques to mentally practice their sports movements. This mental rehearsal can lead to improved actual performance.

Learning and Problem-Solving: Visualization can also aid in learning and problem-solving. When you visualize a complex problem, you can mentally manipulate and experiment with potential solutions. This can lead to better understanding and more effective problem-solving when you encounter similar situations in reality.

Reducing Anxiety: Visualization can help reduce anxiety and increase confidence. For instance, someone anxious about public speaking can mentally rehearse a successful speech, which can boost their self-assurance when they step on the stage.

Sport Psychology Example:

Imagine you're a golfer looking to improve your putting skills. You could use visual imagery in the following way:

Relaxation: Find a quiet, comfortable space to sit or lie down. Close your eyes and take a few deep breaths to relax your body and mind.

Visualization: Begin to mentally picture yourself on the golf course, standing at the putting green.

Detailed Imagery: Imagine the texture of the grass beneath your feet, the feel of the putter in your hands, and the sound of the ball hitting the clubface. Visualize the entire putting stroke, from the backswing to the follow-through.

Outcome Focus: Most importantly, imagine the ball rolling smoothly into the hole with precision. Visualize this happening consistently with each putt.

Repeat: Practice this mental imagery regularly, ideally before actual putting practice or even during breaks throughout the day.

Visual imagery is a powerful psychological technique that can aid in skill development, learning, problem-solving, and even anxiety reduction. It's a valuable tool that individuals, including athletes, students, and professionals, can use to enhance their performance in various domains.

Related Information on The All About Psychology Website

www.all-about-psychology.com/sport_psychology.html

Dark Humor

Why do so many people use dark humor, even though they know it might cause upset and offence?

There are a number of psychological and social factors that may explain the use of dark humor. These include:

Coping Mechanism: Dark humor often serves as a coping mechanism in response to distressing or uncomfortable situations. Humor, in general, can help people manage stress and anxiety. Dark humor allows individuals to address challenging topics in a way that provides emotional distance and relief.

Taboo and Social Norms: Humor frequently arises from breaking social norms or addressing taboo subjects. The act of transgressing social boundaries through humor can be appealing because it feels rebellious or subversive. People may use dark humor to challenge conventions or express their non-conformity.

Relatability: Dark humor can resonate with individuals who have similar experiences or thoughts but might not express them openly. When someone shares a dark joke, it can create a sense of belonging or shared understanding among those who relate to the underlying sentiment.

Catharsis: Dark humor can provide a form of emotional catharsis, allowing individuals to release pent-up emotions or thoughts in a non-harmful way. Laughing at something dark can alleviate tension and provide temporary relief.

Desensitization: Exposure to dark humor over time can lead to desensitization. When individuals are repeatedly exposed to jokes on sensitive topics, they may become less emotionally reactive to them. This desensitization can make it easier to engage in and appreciate dark humor.

Attention-Seeking: Some individuals use dark humor as a means of drawing attention or provoking reactions from others. It can be a way to establish oneself as unique or memorable in social interactions.

Ingroup vs. Outgroup: Dark humor often functions differently within ingroups (those who share similar values and beliefs) compared to outgroups (those who do not). Jokes that might be offensive to outsiders can reinforce bonds among ingroup members, creating a sense of camaraderie.

Social Commentary: Dark humor can serve as a form of social commentary, critiquing societal issues or injustices. It allows individuals to shed light on sensitive topics and provoke discussions about them.

Personality Traits: Research has found that certain personality traits (e.g., extraversion) are associated with the humor styles that individuals tend to employ.

It's important to note that the acceptability of dark humor varies widely depending on cultural, social, and individual factors. What one person finds funny and acceptable; another may find offensive. This diversity of perspectives can lead to misunderstandings and conflicts.

The use of dark humor is complex and can have both positive and negative consequences, depending on the context and the audience.

Related Information on The All About Psychology Website

www.all-about-psychology.com/the-dark-side-of-humor.html

Fascinating research paper on DSM-5 Pathological Personality Traits and Humor Styles.

Is Being a Fantasist Harmful

I have an older brother (50 years of age) who makes up fantastic stories about past glory days. He seems to fantasize about things he wishes he had done/been, and finally reaches a point where he becomes bold enough to tell the fantasy to other family members.

Two components: a) he never tells these stories to anyone other than immediate family, and then only in one on one settings. b) His fantasies are always things that almost could have been. He doesn't ever seem to tell lies that can be easily disproven, like saying, "I was the winning pitcher at the 1974 Little League World Series, a researchable fact; more like, When I was 16, I raced motocross races every weekend and never lost a race. The Parents didn't allow it so I had to sneak out and race under a different name.

MY QUESTION: Is this harmful? He doesn't seem to be doing anything more than embarrassing the person he is telling the story to; is it harmful to him though?

The behavior you've described, where your older brother creates and shares fantastical stories about past achievements or experiences that never happened, falls under the category of what psychologists often refer to as "confabulation" or "fantasy-prone personality." It's important to approach this behavior with empathy and understanding, as there can be various underlying reasons for it, and the impact can differ from person to person.

Here are some possible insights into your brother's behavior:

Coping Mechanism: Confabulation or creating such stories might serve as a coping mechanism for your brother. People sometimes engage in this behavior as a way to manage feelings of inadequacy, low self-esteem, or unmet personal aspirations. By constructing these narratives, they may temporarily boost their self-esteem or feel more significant.

Seeking Validation: Your brother's need to share these stories with immediate family members one-on-one could indicate a desire for validation or approval. These stories might be his way of seeking recognition or attention from those closest to him.

Memory Distortion: It's essential to consider that your brother might genuinely believe these stories due to memory distortion. Memory can be a complex and malleable process, and people may genuinely remember events differently from how they occurred.

Emotional Impact: Whether this behavior is harmful depends on its impact on your brother's well-being and relationships. If he becomes overly invested in these fantasies to the detriment of his real-life goals and relationships, it could be problematic. Additionally, if these stories lead to conflicts or strained relationships within the family, it may be worth addressing.

Understanding and Support: If you're concerned about your brother's behavior, consider having an open and non-confrontational conversation with him. Express your care and concern for his well-being and ask if there's a reason behind these stories. Encourage him to share his thoughts and feelings, and consider suggesting professional support, such as counseling, if needed.

Respect Boundaries: While it's important to be empathetic and supportive, it's also crucial to respect your brother's boundaries. If he is not receptive to discussing the issue or seeking help, you can only offer your understanding and support but cannot force change.

Your brother's behavior might not necessarily be harmful in itself, but it could be indicative of underlying emotional needs or coping strategies. Approach the situation with empathy and a desire to understand his perspective, and consider seeking professional guidance if you believe it could be negatively affecting his life or relationships.

Solastalgia

What Is Solastalgia?

Solastalgia is a relatively new concept in the field of psychology, particularly environmental psychology. The term was coined by Australian environmental philosopher Glenn Albrecht in 2003, it describes a form of psychological distress or existential unease that arises from the emotional or existential disconnect between a person and their changing or degraded environment. Solastalgia is often associated with the experience of witnessing environmental changes, degradation, or destruction in one's home or familiar surroundings.

Here are some key points about solastalgia:

Environmental Change: Solastalgia is triggered by significant environmental changes or disruptions, such as deforestation, urbanization, pollution, climate change, or natural disasters, that affect the place where a person resides or has a deep emotional connection.

Emotional Distress: Unlike traditional forms of homesickness or nostalgia, which are triggered by physical absence from a familiar place, solastalgia is primarily an emotional and psychological distress experienced while still residing in the changing environment. It's a feeling of homesickness without leaving home.

Sense of Loss: People experiencing solastalgia often report a profound sense of loss, grief, anxiety, or even depression. They may mourn the changes to their environment and the associated loss of familiar landscapes, ecosystems, and a way of life.

Connection to Place: Solastalgia highlights the strong emotional connection humans have to their environment and the impact that environmental changes can have on mental well-being. It emphasizes the importance of place attachment in understanding psychological responses to environmental disruption.

Community and Collective Experience: Solastalgia is not limited to individual experiences. Entire communities or regions can collectively experience solastalgia when confronted with large-scale environmental changes, such as the impacts of mining, deforestation, or climate-related events.

Environmental Activism: Solastalgia can also serve as a motivator for environmental activism and conservation efforts. It can inspire individuals and communities to take action to protect their environment and advocate for sustainable practices.

In summary then, solastalgia is a term that describes the emotional distress experienced when individuals or communities witness and feel the impacts of environmental changes and degradation in their familiar surroundings. It underscores the complex relationship between humans and their environment, highlighting the psychological toll of environmental disruption and the importance of addressing these issues in the context of mental health and well-being.

Exploding Head Syndrome

What Is Exploding Head Syndrome?

Exploding Head Syndrome (EHS) is a relatively rare but intriguing phenomenon classified under the umbrella of parasomnias, which are abnormal behaviors or experiences that occur during sleep. EHS is characterized by sudden and vivid auditory hallucinations of loud noises, such as explosions, gunshots, or crashing sounds, which occur when a person is falling asleep or waking up. These noises are not associated with any actual external events but are experienced as real and extremely loud in the individual's perception.

Key Elements of Exploding Head Syndrome include:

Auditory Hallucinations: EHS is primarily an auditory phenomenon, with individuals reporting loud and often terrifying sounds. These sounds can vary in intensity and character but are typically perceived as occurring within the head.

Timing: EHS episodes usually occur during the transition between wakefulness and sleep, either as a person is falling asleep or waking up. They are often accompanied by a brief sensation of fear or dread.

Visual and Sensory Components: In some cases, individuals may also report visual or sensory components accompanying the auditory hallucinations, such as flashes of light or tingling sensations.

While Exploding Head Syndrome itself is considered a neurological sleep disorder rather than a psychological or paranormal phenomenon, its vivid and startling nature can result in some individuals interpreting their experiences in paranormal or supernatural terms. They might, for example, attribute the loud noises to supernatural entities, aliens, or otherworldly events.

With this in mind, it's important to differentiate between the sleep disorder itself and any beliefs or interpretations people may attach to their experiences. The neurological basis of EHS is still not entirely understood, but it appears to involve a disruption in the brain's sleep-wake cycle and auditory processing during the transitional phases of sleep.

To reiterate then, Exploding Head Syndrome is a sleep disorder characterized by sudden and loud auditory hallucinations that occur during the transition between wakefulness and sleep. While some individuals may interpret their EHS experiences as paranormal, the phenomenon itself is generally considered a neurological sleep disturbance.

Related Information on The All About Psychology Website

www.all-about-psychology.com/what-lies-behind-ghosts-demons-and-aliens-according-to-sleep-researchers.html

Fascinating article on sleep paralysis and exploding head syndrome by Alice M Gregory, Professor of Psychology, Goldsmiths, University of London.

Psychology of Conspiracy Theories

Why do so many people believe in conspiracy theories?

Belief in conspiracy theories is a complex phenomenon rooted in various psychological, social, and cognitive factors. Some of the reasons believe in conspiracy theories, include:

1. Cognitive Biases: Human brains are susceptible to cognitive biases, which are systematic patterns of deviation from norm or rationality in judgment. Several cognitive biases contribute to belief in conspiracy theories. For example:

Confirmation Bias: People tend to seek and interpret information in ways that confirm their preexisting beliefs. In the context of conspiracy theories, individuals selectively accept and remember information that supports the conspiracy while dismissing contrary evidence.

Pattern Recognition: Humans are natural pattern-seeking creatures. We often see connections and patterns where they may not exist, leading to the perception of hidden or secret agendas.

2. Uncertainty and Anxiety: Conspiracy theories can provide a sense of structure and certainty in a world that can sometimes seem chaotic and uncertain. They offer simple, black-and-white explanations for complex events, reducing anxiety and ambiguity.

3. Social Identity and Belonging: Believing in a conspiracy theory can be a way for individuals to align themselves with like-minded groups. It can foster a sense of belonging and identity, especially in an age of online communities where conspiracy theories can spread rapidly.

4. Distrust in Authorities: A history of government or institutional misconduct, such as the Watergate scandal or unethical medical experiments like the Tuskegee Study, has eroded trust in official narratives. This distrust can make people more receptive to alternative explanations.

5. Cognitive Dissonance Reduction: When people encounter information that contradicts their beliefs or worldview, they may experience cognitive dissonance, a psychological discomfort. Believing in a conspiracy theory can resolve this dissonance by offering an alternative explanation that aligns with their existing beliefs.

6. Media Consumption: The information ecosystem, including social media and online platforms, plays a significant role in the spread and reinforcement of conspiracy theories. Algorithms can promote content that aligns with users' existing views, creating echo chambers.

One well-known conspiracy theory is the "9/11 Truth Movement," which claims that the U.S. government was involved in or allowed the terrorist attacks on September 11, 2001, to happen. This theory has gained traction due to distrust in government actions and institutions, as well as the complexity of the events, which can make it challenging for some to accept the official account.

It's important to remember that not everyone who believes in conspiracy theories does so for the same reasons, and beliefs can vary widely. Addressing belief in conspiracy theories often requires a nuanced approach, including education, critical thinking skills, and efforts to rebuild trust in credible sources of information.

Memory Echoes

I experience what I can only describe as 'memory echoes, where I get a strong feeling of 'didn't I do this before?' when recalling a memory. Most often the next day. For example, I'll do something completely new, for the first time ever. At the time I know that I've not done it before. However, the next day, when remembering the previous day, I'll be convinced that I've actually done that thing many times before.

I can kind of stop this happening by thinking very 'loudly' to myself 'this is NEW', but even then I sometimes get confused and wonder if maybe I've just forgotten the previous experiences, because the feeling similar to Déjà vu, that I've 'been there, done that', is very strong.

While this condition doesn't really affect me adversely, I'm curious to learn what might be the cause. I'd, therefore, be grateful for any insights.

The experience you're describing as "memory echoes" or a sense of déjà vu, is a curious and intriguing phenomenon. While it is impossible to point to a definitive cause, the following information may offer some insights into the potential causes and factors contributing to the sensation you feel.

Neurological Factors: Déjà vu and similar phenomena are thought to be related to how memories are processed in the brain. Some researchers believe that déjà vu occurs when there is a momentary delay or mismatch in the brain's processing of incoming sensory information and the retrieval of related memories. This can create the sensation that you've experienced something before, even if you haven't.

Memory Consolidation: Memory is a complex process, and sometimes, our brains may consolidate or integrate new experiences with existing memories in unusual ways. This can result in a sense of familiarity with a recent experience, even when it's genuinely novel.

Stress and Fatigue: Stress, fatigue, or altered states of consciousness can affect memory and perception. When you're tired or stressed, your cognitive processes may not function optimally, which can lead to distortions in how you perceive and remember events.

Cognitive Processes: The act of recalling a memory can be a reconstruction rather than a verbatim playback of the original event. During this reconstruction, your brain may inadvertently introduce elements from other memories, leading to a feeling of familiarity.

Psychological Factors: Your emotional state and psychological factors may also play a role. For example, high levels of anxiety or emotional arousal can impact memory and perception.

Individual Variability: It's worth noting that memory processes can vary widely among individuals. Some people may be more prone to experiencing déjà vu or memory echoes due to their unique cognitive and neurological profiles.

If this experience is not causing you distress or interfering significantly with your daily life, it may simply be a quirk of how your brain processes and recalls memories. However, if you find that these experiences become more frequent, distressing, or disruptive, it could be beneficial to consult with a qualified mental health professional or neurologist. They can provide a more in-depth assessment and explore potential interventions or strategies to manage these sensations.

Related Information on The All About Psychology Website

www.all-about-psychology.com/what-is-deja-vu.html

Informative answer to the question what is déjà vu? by Anne Cleary, Professor of Cognitive Psychology, Colorado State University.

Superiority Complex

Whenever I meet someone for the first time, especially if they are the same gender, I always "size them up". I always want to think that they are somehow inferior to me, even though I am clueless as to who they are, or what they are all about.

It seems like I am competing with them for something, but there is nothing to compete for because I don't know them and they don't know me. It not until I actually speak to them and get to know them that my feeling for them changes. Is this normal?

Is there something wrong with me? Is it because I am insecure or afraid that others are better than me?

What you're describing is a common human experience, and it's rooted in psychological processes that have evolved over time. While sizing up or initially making judgments about others may seem negative, it's a natural part of our social cognition, and it doesn't necessarily indicate something wrong with you. Here are some insights into why this happens:

1. Evolutionary Perspective: Humans have evolved to be social creatures, and throughout our evolutionary history, we've had to assess potential threats and alliances quickly. This instinctual behavior helped our ancestors make rapid decisions about whether to trust or be cautious around unfamiliar individuals.

This tendency to assess others quickly, often referred to as "snap judgments," is a survival mechanism.

2. Ingroup-Outgroup Bias: Psychologically, we tend to categorize people as part of our "ingroup" (those we identify with) or our "outgroup" (those we see as different or potentially competitive). This categorization can trigger initial assessments or judgments, although these assessments are often based on stereotypes and limited information.

3. Cognitive Biases: Various cognitive biases, such as confirmation bias (seeking information that confirms our initial judgments) and the fundamental attribution error (attributing behavior to internal characteristics rather than external circumstances), can influence our initial perceptions of others.

4. Social Comparison: The desire to assess oneself in comparison to others is a fundamental aspect of human social behavior. It can be driven by the need to establish one's identity, self-esteem, and sense of belonging.

5. Insecurity and Self-Esteem: In some cases, feelings of insecurity or low self-esteem can amplify these initial judgments and competitive feelings. When we don't feel secure about ourselves, we may unconsciously seek to boost our self-esteem by comparing ourselves favorably to others.

The key takeaway here is that while these initial assessments are common and have evolutionary roots, they don't necessarily reflect your true feelings or intentions. Once you engage in conversation and get to know someone, your perceptions often change, as you mentioned. This transition from initial judgment to a more nuanced and empathetic understanding is a sign of your capacity for social adaptation and empathy.

If you find that these initial judgments are causing distress or impacting your relationships negatively, you can work on being more mindful of your first impressions and consciously challenging any negative or competitive thoughts. Remember that everyone has their unique strengths and qualities, and getting to know others on a deeper level can reveal their full humanity beyond initial impressions.

If you're concerned about feelings of insecurity or self-esteem, it can be helpful to explore these feelings with a mental health professional. They can provide strategies to build self-confidence and navigate social interactions more comfortably. Ultimately, understanding and addressing these tendencies can lead to more positive and fulfilling social interactions.

Afterword

Thank you so much for choosing to explore the world of psychology with me through "Psychology Q & A: Great Answers to Fascinating Psychology Questions." As with all my books, this one was born from a deep passion for psychology and a commitment to making this captivating field accessible to everyone, regardless of their level of expertise or familiarity with the subject.

I hope you found the questions and answers within these pages enlightening and thought-provoking. Psychology, after all, is not just a subject to be studied; it's a lens through which we can better understand ourselves and the world around us.

I encourage you to keep nurturing your curiosity, to keep asking questions, and to keep seeking answers. The journey of learning psychology never truly ends, not least because insights into the human mind and behavior remain an infinite source of wonder.

If you enjoyed this book, please consider leaving a review on Amazon. Your feedback is invaluable and helps others discover the world of psychology through these pages.

Also By

Discover more captivating insights into the world of psychology by exploring David Webb's other published titles, including:

70 Classic Aphorisms And Maxims All Psychology Students Should Know (And Everybody Else For That Matter) - www.amazon.com/Classic-Aphorisms-Psychology-Students-Everybody-ebook/dp/B00SBI4JGO

A Psychological Analysis of Adolf Hitler - www.amazon.com/dp/1481110853

ADHD Planner for Adults: Get Organized, Focus Your Attention and Prioritize Tasks, One Day at a Time - www.amazon.com/dp/B0CFWVZ2LR

Classic Insights into Life and Human Behavior (3 book series) - www.amazon.com/dp/B075V52N5K

On This Day in Psychology: A Showcase of Great Pioneers and Defining Moments - www.amazon.com/This-Day-Psychology-Showcase-Pioneers-ebook/dp/B00V5D0KXI

Psychology Classics: A must-read collection of some of the most famous psychology studies of all time - www.amazon.com/shop/psychologyonline/list/354SK8QUTBZU9

Psychology Scrapbook Volume 1: A Collection of Really Interesting Stuff for Psychology Lovers - www.amazon.com/Psychology-Scrapbook-Collection-Really-Interesting-ebook/dp/B00JXNCMVU

Psychology Student Guide - www.amazon.com/Psychology-Student-Guide-David-Webb-ebook/dp/B009ZC2UOS

Psychology Word Search Puzzles: The Fun Way To Learn All About Human Behavior - www.amazon.com/gp/product/B0915HG2F1

The Incredibly Interesting Psychology Book - www.amazon.com/Incredibly-Interesting-Psychology-Book/dp/1484953991

www.ingramcontent.com/pod-product-compliance
Lightning Source LLC
Chambersburg PA
CBHW070804260726
48660CB00005B/1701